BECOMING A LIFELINE FOR THOSE WHO NEED HOPE

CALLED TO GREATNESS

RON HUTCHCRAFT

This Billy Graham Evangelistic Association
special edition is published with permission
from the publisher, Moody Press.

MOODY PRESS
CHICAGO

All Scripture quotations are taken from the *Holy Bible, New International Version*®. NIV®. Copyright © 1973, 1978, 1984 by International Bible Society. Used by permission of Zondervan Publishing House. All rights reserved.

The "NIV" and "New International Version" trademarks are registered in the United States Patent and Trademark Office by International Bible Society. Use of either trademark requires permission of International Bible Society.

Library of Congress Cataloging-in-Publication Data

Hutchcraft, Ronald
    Called to greatness / Ron Hutchcraft
        p. cm.
    Includes bibliographical references.
    ISBN 0-913367-32-X (Previously ISBN 0-8024-3647-1)
    1. Evangelistic work. I. Title.

Printed in the United States of America

Anybody who has been on the receiving end of Ron Hutchcraft's ministry knows the impact of both his life and his words. In *Called to Greatness* he nags at our conscience one more time. This time about something very close to the heart of Jesus . . . compassion in action. You need to read this book!

Joseph M. Stowell
President
Moody Bible Institute

CALLED TO GREATNESS may be the best evangelism-training manual I have ever seen! Ron gives us the rich distillation of his years doing it in the trenches. His insights are fresh, compelling, liberating, motivating, empowering . . . in other words, priceless. In an easy to apply, easy to pass along approach, Ron has anticipated my major questions, my greatest fears and my deepest longings. No question about it: He's given me A LOT to pray about, and to expect God to do through me!

David Brayant
Founder and President
Concerts of Prayer International

This book is excellent, inspiring, captivating, and full of practical and godly wisdom. It is an outstanding guidebook for Christians seeking God's high calling for their lives—reaching the lost, for whom Christ died.

Steve Douglass
President
Campus Crusade for Christ International

In *Called to Greatness,* Ron Hutchcraft is sharing the passion of his heart, becoming a spiritual lifeline. Christ has called us all to be witnesses; Ron understands this and shares it in his book. With over ninety percent of our population believing in a god of some sort, God is calling His church today to become the lifelines to those in need. There is no greater calling than pitching the saving truth of Jesus Christ to others. Ron Hutchcraft shows how one can rise to the greatest calling and do this with ease. Anyone reading this book will not only understand how to share the greatest story of all but also how to do it in such a way that fear is lessened, and the desire to do so is enhanced.

Tom Phillips
President/CEO
International Students, Inc.

It's about time! With passion and practicality, Ron Hutchcraft puts the cookies on the bottom shelf to help us draw those without Christ into a relationship with Him. This book breaks down emotional barriers so that new believers can truly "taste and see that the Lord is good."

June Hunt
Founder
Hope for the Heart Ministry

Ron Hutchcraft's new book, *Called to Greatness: Becoming a Lifeline for Those Who Need Hope,* is a refreshing treatment of the many challenges Christians face every day. In Ron's practical yet profound treatment of these issues, he takes biblical truths and sheds insight to the daily experiences of Christians. As he addresses these everyday issues, Ron continually magnifies the grace, mercy and loving provision of our heavenly Father for our daily needs. Reading this book by Ron Hutchcraft provides the reader with numerous reminders that the lives of Christians do have divine purpose, order and direction. We live in the balance from a perspective of faith and obedience by the empowering of the Holy Spirit. Under this guidance comes the biblical truth that all of us can rise above the daily challenges to experience hope and fulfill the purpose for which our Lord placed us on the earth! We can both experience the abundant life Jesus Christ gives, and we can model the joy and proclaim the availability of this eternal life to those desiring a personal relationship with Jesus Christ.

Richard H. Harris
Vice President, Church Planting
North American Mission Board, SBC

Ron Hutchcraft has done it again. He is one of the finest Christian communicators of our day. I believe that every Christian who wants to be used of God to the max will be encouraged and helped greatly by this remarkable book.

Paul Cedar
Chairman
Mission America

To my precious wife, Karen,
whose love, integrity, and spiritual passion
have helped me see so much through heaven's eyes;
and to our heroes, our children,
Lisa (and Rick), Doug (and Anna), and Brad,
who have carried His flame into the next generation.

CONTENTS

Introduction
STILL HUNGRY

Some days I take my lunch. Some days I order out for lunch. And on rare occasions, I go home for lunch. This was one of those days.

To be fair, I gave my wife, Karen, no warning. To be honest, I should have. When I asked her what there was for lunch, she answered matter-of-factly, "A hot dog." I was hoping for more. "Are there a *couple* of hot dogs?" She repeated the menu: "A hot dog."

"With a bun, right?"

Patiently, but firmly, Karen gave me the bottom line one more time: "A hot dog."

My last hope was the bag of corn chips that had been in the cupboard the night before. I checked. They were gone. My son and his friends had eaten them all—including the bag, I think.

So lunch that day was a lonely hot dog on a bare plate. I ate everything that was offered to me that day. But when I left, I was still hungry.

That is a feeling many of us know all too well—spiritually, that is. We're eating everything that is offered to us spiritually. We go to all the Christian meetings; we believe all the Christian beliefs; we listen to all the Christian messages; we try to do all the Christian things. But like me on the day of the one hot dog, *we are still hungry*—hungry for something more "filling," more challenging, more powerful.

THE SEARCH FOR SOMETHING MORE

My friend Don is more successful in his business than ever, more involved with his family than ever, more active in serving God than ever. He attends the most thriving church in his area. But in his heart he feels restless. Recently he bluntly summed up that feeling. "I'm just sick and tired of the status quo," he told me. "There's got to be *more*."

That is a restlessness many of us are feeling. Our life is *full*—maybe very full—but it's not *fulfilling*. There is this haunting hollowness inside that is hungry for something that is missing in all our Christianness. Like Don, we're "sick and tired of the status quo." We're ready for something more.

Most of us have lived long enough to realize that "earth stuff" can never be enough to satisfy our soul or give our lives a sense of personal destiny. The hunger for "something more" is intensified every time we reach a goal we thought would make us fulfilled, only to discover that we are still hungry.

For Gwen, that goal was to get her Ph.D. degree and become a psychiatrist. She pursued her dream tenaciously, earned that degree, and is now living her dream as a Christian in the mental health field. But last month she confided one problem with her "dream": "I'm just not enjoying being a psychiatrist," she told me. Gwen is not alone. Many who thought the achieving of a major career goal would be ultimately fulfilling have come up surprisingly restless at the top of their personal "Mount Everest."

A few years ago Ken Hatfield, then football coach at the University of Arkansas, spoke at a Billy Graham Crusade. I remember vividly his testimony of disappointment at the top. In 1964, Ken Hatfield had been a player for Arkansas when they beat Nebraska for the national championship. He told of how he picked up the newspaper the morning after the game and read the headline he had dreamed of: "Arkansas #1!" He then told the crusade crowd, "At the moment of my greatest achievement, I was so depressed." I have not forgotten his four-word explanation: "My god had died."

So often, we pour ourselves into achieving a career goal or a personal goal, only to find ourselves with the goal in hand and still deeply unsatisfied.

Some of us make achieving some level of financial security one of life's major quests. "All my life I thought if I had $10,000 in the bank, I'd feel satisfied and successful," my friend Roger said recently. "I've got a lot more than that now. That's not it." Clearly having financial security does little to answer the "something more" cry of our souls.

Our pursuit of personal fulfillment and significance goes far beyond just material goals, though. We hope for—and, to differing degrees, find—*emotional* success to make our lives complete. From the first human being, God said, "It is not good for the man to be alone" (Genesis 2:18). We were created for relationship, so we put many of our emotional "eggs" in the "basket" of loving relationships. And there is no doubt that strong friendships, a healthy marriage, and a close family help complete us, just as God intended. New vistas of human closeness open up for us when we come to Christ and also discover the fellowship of those who belong to Him. For many, the church becomes a spiritual "nest" where we can find safety and growth in the fellowship of God's people.

The status quo my friend says he is "sick and tired of " is not an unpleasant status quo: great family, great church, great business. Like him, many of your pursuits—educational, financial, emotional, spiritual—may bring you real joy, real pleasure, even satisfaction. But it's just not *enough*. Not enough to quiet the restlessness in your soul. Not enough to give you that sense of legacy, of destiny, of significance that every human soul is wired for.

Even a position of Christian *leadership* may not satisfy the hunger for that "something more." In fact, many Christian leaders today feel that same unexplainable restlessness that stirs the hearts of everyday believers. I have talked with many of them, and they, too, are ready to move beyond spiritual "business as usual."

"NEVER MORE FULFILLED"

Immediately after his graduation from a Christian college, our son Doug went to the southwestern United States to begin a ministry to the young people of a very remote Native American tribe. Since his missionary support had only started to come in, he had little money to work with. His first "bed" was a table in a tiny church storeroom—he said he preferred the table to the floor because of the little "critters" he would have to share the floor with. It is hard to describe the sense of isolation he felt geographically, socially, and spiritually.

We will never forget the call we got from him early one morning, about two weeks into his new life. He had driven eight miles to get to a phone, and he was watching the sun rise as he talked to us. We were eager to know how he was doing. He was his usual straightforward in telling us.

"Mom and Dad—when I was in college, I could get money together when I needed it," Doug said. "I had friends all around me; I had a girl (whom he had broken up with because she was admittedly not ready to share his calling). Basically, I was comfortable." Our parents' hearts ached as he went on to say, "In some ways, I've never felt as alone as I do now." But what followed is what amazed us. "I have none of what I had before— but that's OK. *I have never been more fulfilled, more at peace, in my life!*"

Our son was experiencing what so many of us are restless for—a deep, deep sense of fulfillment and peace about our lives. We want our lives to really *matter*, to really count, to make the greatest possible difference.

A LIFE OF GREATNESS

There is, in every human soul, the need to be part of something much bigger than any earth achievement, or even any earth relationship, can offer. We aspire to a life of *greatness, lasting* greatness. Last year's champion is soon forgotten in the wake of this year's hero. The name on the door of your office is replaced in minutes with the name of your successor. The children you revolve your life around seem to need you less and less with every passing year. The excitement of getting what you always wanted is soon replaced by the desire for something bigger or better.

Today's front-page "star" will soon be tomorrow's page-twenty footnote. One unsettling word hangs over all those earth-things that give our lives some sense of greatness: *temporary*. No friendship, no championship, no scholarship, no relationship, no ownership, no fellowship can fully satisfy our God-given hunger for something that will be great *forever*.

In his famous poem "The Hollow Men," T. S. Eliot concludes with these troubling words:

> *This is the way the world ends*
> *Not with a bang but with a whimper.*

That is exactly how we do *not* want the rest of our years on earth to be—a whimper rather than a bang. Our hearts are yearning for a future that is truly great, great in God's eyes.

Our "sick and tired of the status quo" feelings are actually a magnet drawing us toward *the greater greatness for which we were created.* Our restlessness is actually a *holy discontentment.* In fact, it is likely that God has made you restless! The Bible says of God's ancient people, "He humbled you, *causing you to hunger* and then feeding you with manna, which neither you nor your fathers had known" (Deuteronomy 8:3, italics added). God made them hungry for the powerful work He was about to bring into their lives. He may be stirring up the same kind of appetite in you, because He wants you so hungry for His "more" that you will pursue it. The people who feel spiritually full and satisfied may never taste the "manna" He has for those who are hungry.

As Mary reflected on God's drafting of her to be the mother of the Messiah, she concluded that "He has filled the hungry with good things" (Luke 1:53). After many years of spiritual heroism, God's great servant Paul said he was still pressing on "to take hold of that for which Christ Jesus took hold of me. Brothers, I do not consider myself yet to have taken hold of it" (Philippians 3:12–13). There is in a healthy Jesus-follower this incurable restlessness, this holy hunger for the rest of what God wants to give us.

If you are one of God's spiritually restless ones right now, there is great news for you: *Restlessness usually precedes a powerful touch of God on a person's life.* God has made you hungry so He can feed you with something much bigger, something much more "filling."

The stirring inside you is, in fact, a spiritual *summons* from your Lord, a summons to a destiny that will make the *rest* of your years the *best* of your years. You are being *called to greatness.* This is greatness by *God's* definition. Answering that call will put you on the superhighway to the "something more" your heart is craving.

BEYOND A SMALL WORLD TO A GREAT VISION

Anyone who has taken their child to Disney World or Disneyland has almost surely been required by Junior or Junietta to ride *the ride*. It's this little boat you take along the winding path of a brightly colored canal.

You are surrounded on all sides by singing dolls representing children from every part of the world. The Japanese kids are singing in their kimonos, the Mexican *muchachos* in their sombreros and serapes, the young Africans in their tribal colors. But no matter what part of the world they are from, they are all singing the same song with the same refrain: "It's a small world, after all." Over and over again they sing, "It's a small world, after all. . . . It's a small, small world."

And it's cute—for a *while*. But after the ninety-third chorus of that little song, I'm ready to *swim* the rest of the way just to get out of that tunnelful of "cute." Inside you are screaming, "I am *sick* of a small, small world!"

Jesus' call to greatness is for those of us who feel that way about our *life*. As busy, as Christian as your life is, it may be feeling more and more like a "small, small world." And you're ready to break out into a larger, more significant future. You're ready for the magnificent obsession that comes from the heart of God and into your heart.

There is a memorable scene in the musical *1776*, set on July 3, 1776, the eve of the signing of America's Declaration of Independence. It was that document, adopted on the Fourth of July by the Continental Congress, that declared the thirteen American colonies free from Great Britain. It was, in essence, the birth of a nation.

But that birth was nearly aborted in the days and hours leading up to signing of the Declaration. The musical portrays the agony of John Adams—ultimately the second President of the United States—over the seeming hopelessness of getting the Declaration passed the following day. The delegations from Pennsylvania and South Carolina are opposed; the Delaware delegation is divided. And John Adams, the patriot, is standing all alone in the hall where the fate of independence will soon be decided. His mood is one of despair.

He steps outside and cries into the night some questions that stirred my soul: "Is anybody there? Does anybody care? Does anyone *see what I see?*"

14

I can almost hear Jesus calling out those words. There is a vision He sees that is missed by most of those who belong to Him. He calls to you and me, "Does anyone see what *I* see?" Those who do see what Jesus sees graduate to greatness.

You may not have seen it before. But if your heart is restless for more, He is about to show it to you.

1
OUT
OF THE
HOLDING
PATTERN

"THOSE WHO LEAD MANY TO RIGHTEOUSNESS
[WILL SHINE] LIKE THE STARS FOR EVER AND EVER."
⌐DANIEL 12:3⌐

I thought I had seen the scenery below me before. The pilot soon confirmed my suspicion: Our flight had been placed in a holding pattern. That meant we were no longer making any forward progress; we were just continuing to circle the ground we had covered before. The repeating scenery confirmed the pilot's words.

You can get tired of being in a holding pattern really fast. Especially if it's your *life* that seems to be in a holding pattern. Like a circling aircraft, your life does not *seem* to be standing still. There is plenty of activity around you. It's just that you aren't really going anywhere. Spiritually, the ground looks all too familiar. And your soul wants more. That's because you were designed for more—much more.

King Solomon opened the door to that "more" in his personal "diary," the Book of Ecclesiastes. In a penetrating insight, Solomon noted that God "has also set eternity in the hearts of men" (Ecclesiastes 3:11).

You and I have *eternity* in our hearts. There is a dimension of you that cannot be fulfilled by anything that will end. You have an appetite from God for that which you can never lose, that which will last forever. Anything else is just too small.

So a life that is filled mostly with earth-stuff and earth-pursuits is going to be patently unsatisfying. Your "small world" restlessness may be your heart's warning light that you have an "eternity deficit," a deficit God is ready and waiting to satisfy. He is waiting to satisfy with a passion you can pursue on earth that will fill you with the excitement of eternality. It is, in fact, the passion which Jesus pursued all the way to the cross.

God has made you restless for more because He wants to *eternalize your life*—to make it count for that which will last forever. And you will never be satisfied with less. So much won't last forever. Your job accomplishments, your home, your bank account, your sports, your "stuff"—none of it will last forever. Our days just fill up with a lot that is un-eternal and, therefore, unfulfilling. And even our discretionary time tends to fill up with trivial pursuits—a numbing bombardment of small talk, the mental "junk food" of TV, innumerable hours of sporting events, entertainment, or being lost in cyberspace.

THE RESTLESS ONES

But amid all the demands and distractions of the un-eternal, there is this quiet but relentless voice crying out, "Give me more; give me something that matters . . . something that will matter *forever*."

And the number of the "restless ones" seems to be growing steadily. Everywhere I go, I meet men and women and young people who answer an eager "yes!" when I ask this question, "Do you ever feel a stirring inside that is saying something like this: *I want to make a greater difference with the rest of my life than I have made until now*"?

That passion to make a greater difference with the rest of your life is from the One who gave you your life . . . who gave His life for you! And only He can satisfy that desire to make a difference. And He will— if you will follow Him into the very eternal pursuit He has made you restless for.

CALLED TO SOMETHING BIGGER

Some people have a very long memory. Then Israeli Prime Minister Yitzhak Rabin sure did in 1991 during the Gulf War. I heard a report of a press conference he held during the time that Iraq was firing Scud missiles into Israel. Most of us who followed the news at that time will never forget the eerie sights of Israeli civilians donning their gas masks at the first sound of a missile alarm.

American President George Bush had asked Israel not to escalate the situation by retaliating against Iraq. At the press conference, a reporter asked Prime Minister Rabin how he felt about the president's request. He paused for a moment, and then with a twinkle in his eye responded, "The last time the Jews listened to a talking Bush, we wandered in the wilderness for forty years!"

Actually, the last time there was a talking bush (the *one* time there was a talking bush), the Jews were liberated from four centuries of Egyptian slavery. The story of Moses' encounter with the Most High at a burning bush is one of the most dramatic moments in biblical history—and a powerful example of how God takes a person from a "small, small world" to a life bigger than he ever dreamed. It is, in many ways, an encounter that God has reenacted with countless believers across hundreds of centuries. It is an encounter He may have been preparing you for with your hungry heart. If you are restless to make a greater difference with the rest of your life, then the story of Moses at the burning bush may be a key that unlocks the door.

The Bible raises the curtain on this life-changing day by telling us that "Moses was tending the flock of Jethro his father-in-law . . . and he led the flock to the far side of the desert and came to Horeb, the mountain of God. There the angel of the Lord appeared to him in flames of fire from within a bush. Moses saw that though the bush was on fire it did not burn up" (Exodus 3:1–2).

With his never-a-vacation responsibilities for the family flock and his family's needs, Moses probably had a full life—but probably not a fulfilling one. He lived in a small, small world. It was safe . . . it was comfortable . . . but it was small. And this day was supposed to be just another day of "more of the same."

Until God showed up and summoned him by name. "When the Lord saw that he had gone over to look, God called to him from within the bush, 'Moses! Moses!' And Moses said, 'Here I am'" (verse 4). Moses had no way of knowing that God was about to blow the lid off his life!

God is still in the life-enlargement business. He comes to people who may, like Moses, have a life full of responsibilities—and a life that is pretty much set on cruise control. Most of us have our career niches, our beliefs are settled, our relationships are staked out; we even have that spot in church where we always sit.

But it's not enough. You have too much "eternity in your heart," so the status quo is not satisfying your need for lasting significance. You need something bigger to capture your heart and give greater meaning to the years you have left.

So God comes to you and, somewhere deep in your heart, He summons you by name. You know He wants you—not just someone, but you—for a larger destiny. Like Moses, the Lord God is inviting you to join Him in a powerful mission. He is about to eternalize your life as never before. And you are about to find what your heart has been hungering for.

THE MAKING OF A HERO

We expect the president of the United States to introduce us to some heroes every year as he delivers his annual State of the Union address to the combined houses of Congress. You can count on it. Several times during his speech, the president will allude to some everyday hero who embodies a point he is making. He drives the point home by having that hero seated in the balcony of the House chamber where he or she is introduced for what is usually a standing ovation.

Behind the scenes, reporters ask presidential aides who the "Skutniks" will be this year. It is a reference to the first such everyday hero introduced by an American president, Lenny Skutnik. Ronald Reagan was president and Lenny Skutnik was just one of thousands of federal workers in Washington, D.C.—until the day Air Florida's flight 90 crashed into the Potomac River.

It was a cold January evening in 1982 when the plane, taking off with passengers headed for sunny Fort Lauderdale, Florida, developed ice on its wings and in its engine—enough to bring the plane down as it tried to clear Washington's 14th Street Bridge. Suddenly, the jet struck the bridge and then fell into the frigid waters of the Potomac. Some passengers managed to get out before the plane sank, and they cried for help as they tried to stay afloat in the icy river.

Lenny Skutnik had just left work, and he was walking nearby. He saw the plane go down . . . he heard the cries of the passengers in the water . . . and he jumped into the river to try to help. Fighting the current and the cold, he managed to save the life of a woman who otherwise would have almost surely died in the Potomac that night. A couple of weeks later, Lenny Skutnik, everyday guy, was introduced as a real American hero on national television by the president of the United States.

CALLED TO BE A RESCUER

In a few moments of courage and self-sacrifice, Lenny Skutnik became something that suddenly gave his life dramatically greater significance. He became a *rescuer.*

That is what God summoned Moses to be. It is what He is summoning *you* to be.

The day God announced Moses would be a hero—a rescuer—He said, "'I have indeed seen the misery of My people in Egypt. I have heard them crying out . . . and I am concerned about their suffering. So I have come down to rescue them'" (Exodus 3:7–8). God, the great Rescuer, the ultimate Deliverer, used Moses to rescue His people. God hears the cries of enslaved and hurting people. That is why He sent Moses to the Jews. It is why He sent His "one and only Son" (John 3:16) to a world He so loves, to sin-slaves like us who were "without hope and without God in the world" (Ephesians 2:12).

I can imagine Moses' reaction as He heard that God was going to "come down to rescue" His suffering people: "Yes! That's awesome! These people aren't going to make it without a rescuer. I'm so glad You're going to change things, Lord!" And then came those shocking words that would change Moses' life forever: "So now, go. *I am sending you*" (Exodus 3:10, italics added). Suddenly, Moses' excited "Hooray!" turned to a stunned "Uh-oh."

God was planning an incredible rescue mission, and He was summoning Moses to join Him in it. The Lord was asking Moses to do what an everyday guy named Lenny did by the Potomac River the day of that awful crash—to hear the cries of dying people, abandon personal safety, and rescue people who would die if he stayed where he was.

It is a sobering picture of the crossroads at which you may be standing. The Lord has heard the cries of people around you who are trying to make life work without a Savior. He has seen their lostness. He has felt their pain and the pain of their families. He knows their incurable loneliness, their quiet desperation, the awful eternity awaiting them—and He has come down to rescue them. But God will rescue the people in your personal world through a personal representative—through His "Moses." That is *you*, and that is me. We are the rescuers God sends into a hurting, desperate world.

And all the stirring in your soul for something bigger, something more, may have been to prepare you for the summons of God to join Him in His rescue mission for the spiritually dying people around you. He is summoning you to be His rescuer!

And, understandably, your reaction might be similar to Moses' reaction on the day He was summoned to significance. "Moses said to God, 'Who am I, that I should go?'" (Exodus 3:11). Fear . . . insecurity . . . inadequacy—a sense that you're not the person for a mission this big.

That's understandable. But the Lord blew away all Moses' excuses and objections when He responded, "Who gave man his mouth? . . . Is it not I, the Lord? Now go; I will help you speak and will teach you what to say" (Exodus 4:11–12). Or, to summarize the conversation:

Moses: Who am I, Lord?

God: That's not the question. Who am *I*, Moses?

This summons from God to join Him in His eternal rescue mission is not about who *you* are; it's about who *God* is and that He promises you as He promised Moses, "I will be with you" (Exodus 3:12). By yourself, you *are* inadequate to help someone get to heaven, to help someone you care about put his or her hand into the hand of Jesus. *It is God's power* that gives otherwise inadequate people supernatural resources to accomplish great things for Him.

The Lord of the universe stands ready to pick up your life and give it a significance, a sense of fulfillment beyond anything you have ever experienced. Your heart has got *eternity* in it . . . and you will not be fulfilled until you know you are making an eternal difference with the one life you have. Remember, *there is no greater difference a person can make than to help someone else be in heaven for all eternity.*

The Lord summons you and me to step up and be His rescuers for some people He died for. Those people in harm's way don't understand that yet; they need you to tell them and show them. In the pages ahead, the *how* of being a spiritual rescuer will become clear and doable. But first comes the *who*. It is you. It is I. It is everyone who has been delivered by a loving God.

God's plaintive question has not changed since the days of the prophet Isaiah: "Who will go?" (Isaiah 6:8).

Deep down in your restless heart, can you hear Him summoning you by name? He has heard the cries of the dying people near you. Listen to His call:

"So now, go . . . I am sending you."

2
YOUR
PERSONAL
TITANIC

RESCUE THOSE BEING LED AWAY TO DEATH;
HOLD BACK THOSE STAGGERING TOWARD SLAUGHTER.
—PROVERBS 24:11—

Titanic. It was a blockbuster movie, an award-winning Broadway show, the subject of best-selling books—and one dramatic, tragic night in history that has intrigued generation after generation.

After all we have heard and seen about the sinking of the "unsinkable" ship, there is still something hauntingly magnetic about her story. In the early twentieth century, the R.M.S. *Titanic* was the crowning achievement of human technology—and yet an iceberg in the north Atlantic Ocean sent her to the bottom in two hours. There may never have been one vessel that carried more of the world's wealthiest and most powerful at one time. Yet the wealth and power were rendered meaningless in a moment by six small gashes in *Titanic's* massive hull.

For the seven hundred survivors—more than 1,500 passengers and crew died—the images of that horrific April night in the North Atlantic are unforgettable. The brightly lit ocean liner sinking lower and lower . . . the futile flares exploding in the sky above the doomed vessel . . . the ship's last agonizing moments with her bow pointing upward, then sliding beneath the water . . . and the sudden near-silence as the ocean erased the *Titanic* from her icy surface.

Moviegoers and book readers will remember those images. But of all the mental pictures of what author Walter Lord called "A Night to Remember," none is more unsettling to me than what happened after the *Titanic* had sunk below the surface. The survivor accounts of that night tell us that there were only twenty lifeboats aboard—about half of what was required to fully evacuate the ship. Most of them were only partially full; some were actually half-empty! As the *Titanic* was sinking, many passengers were able to put on a lifejacket, but they could not find an available lifeboat. They jumped or fell into the ocean, left floating in the frigid waters, crying into the night for help.

Again, there was room in the lifeboats for hundreds of them! That is why their fate is perhaps the most shocking human tragedy of that heartrending night when 1,500 people died. Though those in the water continued to cry out for someone to rescue them, the people in the lifeboats just kept rowing away. They thought rescue was too risky. So out of those twenty lifeboats, *only one finally turned back,* in time to save only six passengers.

Three days later when the funeral ships arrived from Nova Scotia, they were greeted by a ghostly sight: 328 lifejacketed men, women, and children, floating in the water, frozen to death. And why did they die? Not because the *Titanic* sank, but because the people who were already saved would not go back for the people who were not.

THE JESUS LIFEBOAT

That image goes through my soul like cold steel. Could this be a spiritual picture of us: the people who are already saved doing nothing about the dying people all around us? By God's grace we are in the Jesus lifeboat, saved and headed for heaven. But all around us—where we work, where we live, where we shop or go to school—are people who will die spiritually unless someone rescues them. Some of them are people you know, people you love, people within your reach.

In a sense, God has placed us close to these spiritually lost and dying people so we might man the lifeboats that give them hope of being rescued. Will we turn our lifeboats around? Will we take the risks to give them a chance to live—forever? The alternative is to just keep rowing —and let them die.

Tragically, too many Christians are content to just enjoy their own safe place in Jesus' lifeboat. We fellowship with our lifeboat comrades, sing our lifeboat songs, and even work on ways to make our lifeboats bigger and more comfortable. Meanwhile, people we see day after day are drowning spiritually, with no understanding that God's one and only Son died so they don't have to.

And they remain unrescued—or even unnoticed—because those of us who are already rescued have *the disease*. I once heard a pro basketball coach describe the disease, which is common to the general public as well as to Christians. Pat Riley had just been named coach of the New York Knicks. The Knicks' record had been pretty sorry, and the new coach attributed it to a disease he said his players had. Coach Riley called it the disease of *me*. Athletes can catch it, but so do many believers, especially those in relatively comfortable situations.

CHRISTIANITY'S DEADLY DISEASE

The reality is that our Christianity has a tendency to become *self-focused* and *self-absorbed*. We are, in a sense, all about us. We want to pile up more blessing on our already overloaded plate. We expect programs that meet *our* needs, a place where *we* feel comfortable, church the way *we* like it. All too often, our notebooks are full of sermon notes, our schedules are full of Christian meetings, our heads are full of Christian beliefs—and our lifeboat is full of empty places where dying people desperately need to be! It's all part of the disease of me.

Offer a seminar or book on how to raise your children, how to manage your money, or how to lose weight and you will have a full house or a best-seller. But offer teaching on how to present Jesus to lost people and you will fill a lot fewer chairs and sell a lot fewer books. It is not that those practical issues of following Christ are not important— they just are not life-or-death issues. Rescuing the spiritually dying is life or death.

You and I have nothing more urgent, more significant to do than to try to get the people we know into the lifeboat before they slip away forever. Recently my friend Troy told me about his best friend who had died instantly in an automobile accident. "What I can't get over is that I never told him about Jesus," he said. Troy was struggling with the eternal consequences of his silence—of where his friend might be now, where he might be forever. Troy's burden was great. At the funeral, we think about whether that person we cared about knew Jesus and what we could have done to change that. We need to be thinking about that *now,* while there is still time.

A complacent, self-focused relationship with Christ is expensive for us and expensive for people we know who are spiritually lost. For us, a faith that is "all about me" and "all about us" (my fellow believers) confines us to a "small, small world." Me-centered Christianity is ultimately boring, unchallenging, and just not enough to satisfy our eternity-starved soul. For the unrescued people around us, our inward focus could cost them heaven.

In a stirring passage where Paul issues a challenge to us to live boldly for Christ and those Christ died for, he says that Christ "died for all, that those who live should no longer live for themselves" (2 Corinthians 5:15). Jesus gave His life so we could finally graduate from living for ourselves. To the extent our life is still focused on our own agenda and comfort, we are missing the point of what Jesus died to make us.

The One we claim to follow surrendered Himself so others could live: "Even the Son of Man did not come to be served, but to serve, and to give His life as a ransom for many" (Mark 10:45). If you are going to follow Jesus, you will be surrendering yourself for those who are spiritually dying.

You won't be able to just keep rowing away. You'll turn your lifeboat around . . . you'll take the risks . . . you'll rescue the dying, whatever it takes.

4-D GLASSES

As a kid, I often rode my bike up to the old theater on 79th Street for the Saturday afternoon "flick." But one particular day, as I walked into the theater with my big box of popcorn, they handed me a pair of glasses. They were strange glasses, made of cardboard with tinted plastic for lenses. But they opened up a revolutionary viewing experience for all of us who put them on during the movie—they called it *3-D,* as in three-dimensional.

Those goofy-looking spectacles actually offered a bold new vision, a whole world where the events in a movie no longer just stayed flat on the screen but leaped off and right into your face. Looking through those glasses, you saw things that you could never see without them.

When Jesus summons you and me to be spiritual rescuers of dying people, He outfits us, in a sense, with a new pair of spiritual "glasses"—not 3-D glasses, but 4-D glasses. They give us the ability to see a fourth dimension in the people around us, to see what Jesus sees: the lostness beneath what's on the surface.

Looking through "the eyes of Jesus," you see things you could never see without them. You see the "eternalness" of your coworkers, your fellow students, your neighbors, your teammates, your friends at school. Your heart is moved as you watch the quiet desperation of them trying another day without a Savior. You're driven to take action to reach them for Jesus because you see them as precious creations of God, headed for an awful eternity without Him. You feel compelled to intervene.

That night when the Titanic's survivors were floating in a frigid ocean, anyone could see those people would die if someone did not rescue them. But the "dyingness" of the people you know is not nearly so evident. Honestly, they often don't look like they're dying. They may be very decent people. They may be religious people, successful people, likable people, physically strong people who seem to "have it all together." If all you can see is what earth-eyes reveal, you will not feel much urgency to tell them about Jesus; you will not feel enough compulsion to take the risks of reaching out. You may not even *think much* about communicating Christ to them. Not hearing any cries, not seeing any life-or-death situation, you can just keep enjoying your comfortable spot in the lifeboat.

The urgency to help will come only when Jesus shows you what *He* sees when He looks at the people in your world. He sees them as they really are. And something happens in His heart. Matthew reported of Christ, "When he saw the crowds, he had compassion on them, because they were harassed and helpless, like sheep without a shepherd" (Matthew 9:36). The Greek word for *compassion* used in the original language of this passage is rooted in the word for *entrails*. When Jesus saw people through His "4-D glasses," something happened way down deep inside His soul. He saw sheep without a shepherd. Wandering with no direction, futilely trying to meet their own needs, those sheep were doomed to starve, to fall over the edge or into the coyote's claws. So Jesus committed His life to rescuing them.

The personal mission statement of the Son of God is summed up in these words: "The Son of Man came to seek and to save what was lost" (Luke 19:10). The word Jesus uses when He says He came to "save" means to rescue from danger, to save from death. Peter used the same word when he was about to drown and cried out desperately, "Lord, save me!" (Matthew 14:30). And the word Jesus uses for the "lost" He has come to save is *apollumi,* which can mean *ruined, destroyed, perishing.* In John 3:16, when God announces He loved us so much that He gave His one and only Son "that whoever believes in him shall not perish," *perish* is from that same word for ruin and destruction. The whole life's work of our Lord is a relentless, passionate, "whatever it takes" effort to "seek and to save" those who are dying.

One day you heard the "follow me" of Jesus, and you said you would. If you are following Jesus, you will be doing what He came to do: You will be rescuing the dying, whatever it takes. If you don't see the life-or-death issue of people's terminal spiritual condition, as Jesus does—if you are not actively, urgently doing something about their lostness, as Jesus does—then you have reason to question whether you are really following Jesus.

In a world addicted to what's comfortable and what's easy and in a Christian culture that is often so inwardly focused, you will not step up to your destiny assignment as a spiritual rescuer until you *see what Jesus sees* when He looks at the lives all around you.

HOW GOD DESCRIBES THOSE WITHOUT HIM— SOME SHOCKING WORDS

Such passion comes from having a Jesus-heart for the people who are part of your world. And the miracle of a Jesus-heart can come only from God Himself. It is not something a sermon or book—yes, even this book—can give us. Nor is it something that comes naturally. What comes naturally is being consumed with what's on *our* own plate and seeing people externally rather than eternally. To have your Lord's perspective on your family, friends, or associates who do not know Christ, begin by absorbing what God says about them. And in His Word, He uses some shocking words to describe those who do not have a personal relationship with Him.

Let's look at some of those words, but not just theologically or intellectually. Let's read these descriptions with a face; attach to these descriptions the name of a lost person you care about.

- "those being led away to death ... those staggering toward slaughter" (Proverbs 24:11)
- "separated ... from your God" (Isaiah 59:2)
- "people living in darkness ... those living in the land of the shadow of death" (Matthew 4:16)
- "lost" (Luke 19:10)
- "condemned already" (John 3:18)
- "Whoever rejects the Son will not see life ... God's wrath remains on him" (John 3:36).
- "those who are perishing" (1 Corinthians 1:18)
- "without hope and without God in the world" (Ephesians 2:12)
- in "the dominion of darkness" (Colossians 1:13)
- "They will be punished with everlasting destruction and shut out from the presence of the Lord" (2 Thessalonians 1:9).
- "those who all their lives were held in slavery by their fear of death" (Hebrews 2:15)
- "thrown into the lake of fire" (Revelation 20:15)

These words are not just about some theological concept—they are describing people you know, anyone who has not been to the cross of Jesus to get their sin forgiven, who is trusting anything or anyone other than Jesus to get them to heaven. You will begin to see what Jesus sees when you put the name of someone you know like that into a heartrending sentence like this:

_____ (name of the person you care about) is being led away to death ... is separated from God ... will not see life ... is under God's wrath ... will be punished with everlasting destruction ... will be shut out from the presence of the Lord ... will be thrown into the lake of fire.

That's what's at stake in this rescue mission. That's what God sees when He looks at the people you care about. When Jesus looks at the people cruising the mall, He doesn't see shoppers—He sees dying people. When Jesus sees young people pouring out of the local school each afternoon, He doesn't see students—He sees dying people. When Jesus watches men and women going into that factory or office building each morning, He doesn't see workers—He sees dying people.

Do you? If you cannot see dying people, you will never follow Jesus into the rescue mission for which He came. Even more, you will never know the unparalleled fulfillment of God using you to help change someone's eternity. And your friends and associates and loved ones will go on dying. To be a spiritual rescuer, you must see the eternal "dyingness" of people you know—to see them as future inhabitants of hell. And to see their peril, you must have a Jesus-heart. That can begin—having the compassionate heart of Jesus—when you would dare to ask God for it. How do you ask? In a simple prayer like this: "Go ahead, God—break my heart for the lost and dying people around me."

Let Jesus plant His love for those He died for in your heart. Let Him plant in you His passion for "not wanting anyone to perish" (2 Peter 3:9). Ask Him to help you feel the awful condition of those who are outside the lifeboat—and to feel the "whatever it takes" urgency of reaching into their night and helping them into the lifeboat. With that kind of heart, God can begin to enlarge your life and to use it for the most eternal purpose a human being can be a part of: getting someone to heaven for all eternity.

God sent His one and only Son to die for the people who are described in such shocking words as "condemned," "perishing," and "shut out." Jesus died so they don't have to. He gave His life so they could become:

- someone who "is not condemned" (John 3:18) and who "has eternal life" (John 3:36)
- a child of God (John 1:12)
- a lost sheep He brings home (Luke 15:6)
- "rescued . . . from the dominion of darkness and brought . . . into the kingdom of the Son he loves" (Colossians 1:13)
- one of those who will "go through the gates into the city" (Revelation 22:14) where "there will be no more death or mourning or crying or pain" (Revelation 21:4)

Those words, too, can describe the people you know and love—if they will come to the cross of Jesus and put their trust in the God-man who died there for all the sinning they have ever done. But first, they have to know and understand that what happened on that cross was for them. And the delivery of that Good News, that life-or-death news, Jesus has entrusted to His followers. He has entrusted it to someone whose lifeboat is already close to the dying people you know. He has entrusted the rescue to you.

THE MOST IMPORTANT
TITLE YOU WILL EVER HAVE

I was the Boone County Spelling Bee champion once. For a little while, I held the title. That was soon forgotten, and someone else held the title. It's that way with everyone, whether you are captain, most valuable player, class speaker, director, president, or "Woman of the Year."

But there is one title, conferred by God, that has incredible eternal significance. It is a title that forever enlarges the significance of the one who carries it. The title does not require a degree, a vote, a bank account, or friends in high places. It belongs to many people who have never held any other title in their lives. If you belong to Jesus Christ, you have already been given this powerful title—and the sobering responsibility that accompanies it.

The announcement of this important position is made in God's Word in 2 Corinthians 5:18–20:

> God [has] reconciled us to himself through Christ and gave us the ministry of reconciliation: that God was reconciling the world to himself in Christ, not counting men's sins against them. And he has committed to us the message of reconciliation. We are therefore Christ's ambassadors, as though God were making his appeal through us. . . . Be reconciled to God.

Ambassador—there is the title that comes with a personal relationship with Jesus Christ. In the world of politics and international relations, the title *ambassador* is a coveted one. In fact, people now serve years in government, and sometimes donate large sums to presidential campaigns, hoping to be rewarded with that title. It is a high honor to be trusted by the government of your nation to be the face and voice of your nation somewhere in the world.

By definition, an ambassador is a person assigned by the highest authority to represent him in a specific place. Usually a nation's president or prime minister appoints the ambassador.

The impression people in that place have of the ambassador's country depends on how the ambassador lives. Whether or not they understand the mind and heart of the one who assigned you depends on how clearly you communicate it by word and deed.

And we are "Christ's ambassadors"! Appointed by the highest Authority in the universe ... to represent *Him*. Talk about significance! "He has committed to us the message" of what He did on the cross. He is counting on us to represent what He is like by the way we live, to communicate clearly the message He gave His life for.

But you have not only been appointed by the highest Authority to represent Him and deliver His message. You have been assigned to represent Him in a specific place: the neighborhood you live in, the school you go to, the place you work, the team you're on, the store where you shop. You are Christ's ambassador right where you are.

Jesus is no longer here in a physical presence. Just as a country's ambassador is somewhere in the world, standing in for his president, you are assigned to your circle of influence to be there "on Christ's behalf." In essence, you know in your heart that "Jesus isn't here right now, folks; He sent me to represent Him."

It is possible you may not want the responsibility of Christ's ambassadorial appointment. It appears you have no choice—you already have the assignment. "We *are* Christ's ambassadors," Paul wrote. By virtue of the fact that you are His man or woman in your circle of influence, people will be forming their opinions of Jesus based on you, for better or worse. They will either understand His life-saving message or miss His message based on what you do or do not say. You may be an effective ambassador for Jesus or you may be a disastrous one—but you will be Christ's ambassador. And someone's eternity may depend on what kind of ambassador you turn out to be.

You have a life-or-death assignment from Jesus: to be His ambassador, to deliver His message. You have a life-or-death mission from Jesus: to be His rescuer, to reach someone who is dying without Him.

It would be overwhelming were it not for the fact that it will be His power working through you, not your doing work for Him. It was God's great ambassador, Paul, who said: "Not that we are competent to claim anything for ourselves, but our competence comes from God"

(2 Corinthians 3:5). If you think you can't do this, you're right. God is asking you to show up ready and prepared; He will take it from there.

The eminent Bible commentator William Barclay recognized that great resource we all have when he wrote of Jesus' sending out of His disciples to reach a lost world—and the accompanying promise (in Matthew 28:19–20) that He would be with them always:

> It must have been a staggering thing for eleven humble Galileans to be sent forth to the conquest of the world. Even as they heard it, their hearts must have failed them. But, no sooner was the command given, than the promise followed. They were sent out—as we are—on the greatest task in history, but with them there was the greatest presence in the world.[1]

"THE LAST ONE I'LL LOSE"

My father-in-law loved to tell many stories about his life; in his later years he told me a story about when he was a boy that I had never heard before. As a boy in Kansas, he had been out playing near the river with some other children. Suddenly, he heard the scream of a girl who had fallen in the water. Not knowing how to rescue a drowning person, he could only watch helplessly as she went under. Dad told me, "I made up my mind that day that something like that was not ever going to happen again; that girl would be the last one I lost." He decided that day that he would do whatever he had to do to learn how to rescue a drowning person.

Dad had one slip away before his eyes. But he kept his commitment—it never happened again. During his lifetime, he was in four situations where someone was drowning, one his own pastor. Four drowning people—all rescued, thanks to him.

Maybe you have watched too many people slip away without knowing the Savior who came to rescue them from their sins. And you can't go back and change that. But you can do what a boy in Kansas did the day he saw someone drown before his eyes. You can make up your mind to do whatever it takes to learn how to rescue dying people. The pages ahead are dedicated to helping you do that.

Jesus is summoning you to join Him in the rescue mission for which He died. No longer will you be content to just occupy a lifeboat and be saved yourself. You have heard the cries of the dying people. And you will not let them go on dying without a chance to live.

3
YOUR
CLEVER
DISGUISE

"I HAVE MADE YOU A WATCHMAN . . . SO HEAR THE WORD
I SPEAK AND GIVE THEM WARNING FROM ME. WHEN I SAY
TO THE WICKED, 'O WICKED MAN, YOU WILL SURELY DIE,'
AND YOU DO NOT SPEAK OUT TO DISSUADE HIM FROM
HIS WAYS, THAT WICKED MAN WILL DIE FOR HIS SIN, AND
I WILL HOLD YOU ACCOUNTABLE FOR HIS BLOOD."

‸EZEKIEL 33:7–8‸

As the senior minister of a megachurch, Pastor Highland could never learn the names of all the people who attended. He knew that, but one day he heard a memorable introduction from Hazel, a weekly regular. As he was shaking hands at the church door, the pastor asked the unfamiliar attendee the get-acquainted question, "What do you do?"

He expected to hear an occupation for an answer. Instead he listened to Hazel's insightful reply. "Oh, pastor," she said, "I'm a disciple of Jesus Christ, cleverly disguised as a machine operator!"

Now there's a lady who knows who she is. Her friends and coworkers would probably just say, "Hazel? Oh, she's a machine operator." To which Hazel might reply, "No! That's just my clever disguise! My job simply puts me in a position to direct other machine operators to Jesus Christ!"

After all, who is a lost machine operator most likely to listen to about a relationship with Jesus? Another machine operator. Who is a lost mom most likely to listen to? Another mom. An unreached businessman will respond best to another businessman, a student to another student, a teacher to another teacher. So, as a follower of Christ, what you do is meant to be your clever disguise that positions you to represent Jesus to people like you in that personal universe.

Once you open your heart to see the lostness of the people around you as Jesus does, once you grasp the life-enlarging ambassadorial assignment God Himself has given you, then you begin to see every aspect of your life more eternally. For example, why do you live where you live? Simple answer: "I liked the neighborhood. I could afford it." Jesus' answer would be: "You live where you live because you have been assigned by Me to be My personal representative to the folks who live there."

Why do you work where you work—just because they hired you? No. You work where you work because *Jesus Christ placed you there to help some of the people there go to heaven with you.* Why do you go to the school you attend? "Because I live in the district?" No again. You go to school where you do because Jesus needed someone to be His personal link to some students there—and you are His chosen ambassador.

DIVINE ASSIGNMENTS

You are divinely assigned to the people in your world, divinely positioned by God as His spiritual rescuer for those around you. Grasp that reality and your everyday activities and relationships will gain great significance. You will be getting a glimpse of the eternal impact you were made for.

You are uniquely positioned—optimally positioned—to introduce the people in your universe to Jesus Christ. The spiritually dying people there are most likely to listen to someone who faces the same kind of pressures they face, someone who lives the same kind of schedule, who knows the same kind of emotions. Someone like you.

My friend Bill has enjoyed uncommon financial success in his life, and he has many "friends in high places." He has often used his connections, not to promote himself, but to promote the Savior who changed his life. That was his intention when he offered to help a woman invite her spiritually lost dad to an upcoming adult outreach.

Her dad was a professor at one of America's military academies, and at that time Bill knew the chairman of the joint chiefs of staff, a leading military figure appointed by the president of the United States. Bill offered to have the chairman (who was a believer) invite this woman's father to the event. And failing that, he would even have a Christian member of the president's cabinet invite Dad. But much to my friend's surprise, the woman said, "No, that won't work." He asked her what would work, who could get through to her father. Her answer was simple and direct: "He'll respond to another professor."

Her father was like most people—they respond best to someone in their world. And in the life-or-death business of spiritual rescue, the best people to do the rescuing are everyday Christians. Not some highly trained religious professional but some believers who, like Peter and John, are considered "ordinary" but have "been with Jesus" (Acts 4:13).

We live during a time where the divide between the world of the church and the world of the unreached person has never been wider, where most lost people either turn off or turn away at the approach of a "minister." It is not "Joe or Joanne Slick" who will most likely break through to a lost heart. It will be "Joe or Joanne Average." Often the person who feels the least qualified to communicate Christ is in the best position to do it. That is why the pages ahead are dedicated to helping the people who are best positioned for rescuing to become confident in how to do it.

ETERNITY ON TOP OF A SEPTIC TANK

Dan has discovered that his business is really his "clever disguise" to get into lives that need his Savior. He could be described as an "underground" Christian: He owns a portable restroom and septic service company. Recently, Dan related to me an unforgettable personal example of how God can use any believer's position to connect someone to Jesus Christ—and how naturally supernatural things can happen.

Dan had loaned a portable restroom to a customer for his wedding. When Dan returned the next weekend to pick up the unit, the customer, Mark, mentioned that he was having a problem with his septic system. Dan agreed to do the repair after he made his last delivery. Mark's newlywed wife, Donna, overheard the offer to return and looked Dan in the eye and said, "God must have sent you here today, because no one helps people anymore."

"Maybe He did," Dan answered.

When Dan came back, he helped Mark thread a metal snake through the sewer line and into his house. It took about an hour, and when the job was done, Dan covered the septic tank. He was standing on top of the lid—right in the middle. Donna again said, "God must have sent you here today, because nobody helps people anymore."

"So you believe in God?" Dan asked. That began a conversation about spiritual things. As he stood on that septic tank, he proceeded to tell Mark and Donna about Jesus.

Donna indicated she had made an earlier commitment to Jesus; Mark seemed much less interested in the conversation. After forty-five minutes of conversation, though, Mark and Donna suggested everyone go to the local diner to talk some more. The conversation continued until they returned to Mark's home.

"I smoke cigarettes," Mark said during the ride back home. "So if I were to die tonight, would I go to heaven?"

"Mark, if another truck came around the corner, hit us, and we all died—and you were smoking cigarettes and had not made a personal commitment to Jesus Christ—you would go to hell," Dan said. "But if that truck hit us and you had just committed your life to Christ and you still had the cigarette in your hand, I believe with all my heart that you would be in heaven. But I don't know about the cigarette!"

The three talked some more and then arrived at the couple's home. Before Dan left, he asked if they would mind if he prayed for them. They agreed, and Dan specifically asked that their hearts would be softened, and that they would both come to a saving knowledge of Jesus Christ. The next day he dropped off a Bible for them to read.

Dan didn't hear from Mark and Donna for about two months. During that time he suffered a life-threatening medical problem that required emergency surgery. He spent two weeks in the hospital and then was sent home to recover. Dan explained what happened next. "It was then I received a phone call from Mark. He told me things weren't going so well with him and Donna. He said they had been thinking about what we had discussed and asked if I would meet with them again. I told him that I needed them to come to my home because I wasn't able to go out.

"They came to my home one evening and we talked for about two hours. Mark didn't have many comments, just question after question.

They came over again. More questions followed. It seemed as though they would continue without end. At one point I left the room to look up an answer to one of Mark's questions. I searched for my Bible that had been marked and even telephoned my pastor and an elder in my church to get the answer, but found both lines busy. I sensed the Lord asking me, 'What are you doing?' In my heart I answered, 'I'm trying to save Mark.' The response was, 'You can't do that. Only I can do that.'

"I got on my knees and confessed my sin and I thanked God for correcting me in that way. I went back into the room where Mark and Donna were sitting and I asked Mark if he had any more questions. He said no. He then said he was ready to confess his sin and believe in Jesus. I quickly fell to my knees and led him in prayer. Today Mark and Donna are married with two children, professing Jesus as Lord and sharing Christ with those around them.

"As for me, I not only gained two great friends, but I also learned that Jesus can be preached from anywhere—even from the top of a septic tank—because it is God who does the saving."

A life-changing miracle for a couple without Christ. It did not begin in a church or at an evangelistic crusade. For most unreached people, it probably never will. They will have to be reached in the middle of their world by a Jesus-follower who is already in their world. Someone like my friend Dan, finding his lifesaving opportunity as he stood on a septic tank. Someone like you during the course of a day's work; in a locker room; in your yard; on a school bus, a commuter train, or a golf course; on a hunting trip or a shopping trip.

The life-saving strategy of Jesus is based on ordinary people showing and telling about Him in ordinary places. That should not surprise us. After all, it is how Jesus Himself did it. He rescued a Samaritan woman at a well where they both had stopped for a drink . . . a tax collector as He passed by his tax office . . . fishermen as He walked along their stretch of the beach . . . Zaccheus over lunch at his house. He changed their eternities because "He made His dwelling among us" (John 1:14). Today He is changing people's eternities through His everyday followers who dwell among men and women He died for. The charge of the Master to His first followers—and to us—is "As the Father has sent Me, *I am sending you*" (John 20:21, italics added).

When you go through your day remembering who you really are—Jesus' ambassador assigned to represent Him—your eyes suddenly see natural opportunities to bring up life's most important relationship. You see them because you're looking for them, you're expecting them, and you're praying for them.

And you can dare to bring Jesus into the lives God entrusts to you because of one liberating fact: It is God who does the saving. You only need to be His glove.

ABANDONING SAFETY

There may be no one in the Bible who better fleshes out why God has you where you are than a Jewish orphan named Esther. In the book that bears her name, she is introduced as living in Persia, where her people have been taken in captivity. There is no way Esther could imagine how she would be suddenly swept into deadly intrigue in the court of the world's most powerful man.

First, the King of Persia, the world's most dominant empire, dethroned his queen and started a nationwide search for a new queen. Amazingly, Esther won the "Miss Persia" pageant and was selected to be the queen; no one in the king's court knew her Jewish heritage. Esther was suddenly propelled into a position where she had all the glamour and all the glory a young woman could want. She was living the dream of every woman in the kingdom.

But later a prominent court official, who hated the Jews, maneuvered the king into signing a proclamation ordering their elimination. Word of the planned holocaust reached Mordecai, the compassionate cousin who raised young Esther. He sent her a desperate message asking her "to go into the king's presence to beg for mercy and plead with him for her people" (Esther 4:8).

Esther fired back a reply reminding Mordecai of what her intervention could cost her. She referred to the Persian law that anyone who approached the king in his court without being summoned must, by law, be put to death. The only exception was for the king to extend his gold scepter and spare the person's life. Esther had reason to question the status of her relationship with the king. "Thirty days have passed since I was called to go to the king," she told Mordecai via her messenger (verse 11).

Mordecai replied with a question that cut right to the central issue of Esther's divine assignment—and right to her heart. Mordecai "sent back this answer: . . . 'Who knows but that you have come to royal position for such a time as this?'" (Esther 4:13–14). This messenger of God seemed to say, "Esther, don't you realize why the Lord has placed you in the position you're in? It's not just so you can enjoy the benefits of being the queen. God has put you where you are so you would be in a position to save lives!"

That is God's message to you, too. You are in that neighborhood, that school, that workplace, that group by God's design—not just to enjoy the benefits of your position, but to be God's instrument to save the lives of the people in that place; to give them the information about Jesus and His cross that can direct them from eternal death to eternal life.

When Esther realized this was a life-or-death situation and that she was in a unique position to do something about it, she made the choice rescuers have made through the centuries: "If I perish, I perish" (verse 16). No life can be rescued if the rescuer chooses to stay where it's safe. You join the rescue work of Jesus when you say to Him, "Lord, I will rescue the dying, whatever it takes—whatever it costs."

Esther made that choice—and God saved the lives of a nation.

THE HIGH PRICE OF STAYING ON SHORE

Jamie's critical choice came one beautiful night several years ago at the New Jersey seashore. She was there as one of our counselors for a youth conference at Ocean City, New Jersey. One of Ocean City's great attractions is its long boardwalk, lit up from one end to another with endless carnival rides, miniature golf courses, quaint shops, and food stands with irresistible treats.

Jamie's defining moment came one night when she left the oceanside auditorium a few minutes before the meeting let out. As she melted into the crowds "cruising the boards," as the locals say, she suddenly heard what she thought was a scream coming from the nearby ocean. Running down the wooden boardwalk stairs, she hurried to the water's edge and peered into the night. This time there was no doubt—she was hearing the screams of a woman somewhere out there in that pitch-black ocean.

Jamie stood there for a moment, almost paralyzed by the choice she knew she had to make. Someone was drowning, and she might have only seconds left to do something. The thought of plunging into the waters of the Atlantic, not knowing what was out there, scared her.

But then she was overtaken by what seemed to be a singular choice. She had to take action. Jamie called up to the crowd cruising the boardwalk, yelling for people to come and help. Then, before she knew if anyone would respond, she pulled off her shoes and plunged into the water. As she swam desperately toward the screams, she was soon joined by a couple of men who had heard her own cry for help.

They reached the drowning woman before she went under and managed to get her back to the beach. Emergency medical personnel were arriving, thanks to others who heard the summons for help. That night a woman's life was saved—a woman who would have died had someone not been willing to take huge risks to rescue her, someone who gave others the same urgency to save a dying woman.

Later, Jamie told me what raced through her mind that night as she stood on the shore, listening to the screams and counting the cost. "I knew how dangerous it would be to go in after her. But there was one thing that mattered more than the danger—someone was going to die if I didn't go in after her."

I am sure Jamie wished there was a lifesaving professional there that night, but there wasn't. If she had waited until someone had come who saved people for a living, the person drowning in the surf would have died. Jamie was the one close enough for the rescue, the person in the position to save this dying person. She could not delegate the responsibility to someone "more qualified." Whether a woman lived or died was in her hands.

You know someone like that, someone who is drowning spiritually, without hope. Perhaps you have thought, "I hope the person comes in contact with one of those trained, professional rescuers some day. There must be someone more qualified than I to fight for her life." Maybe so. But there is no one like that in the life of some dying person you know. But you are in his or her life. If the person never goes to a Christian meeting, if she never hears a message from a trained communicator, you're there. You have Jesus by one hand and that dying person by the other. You are the one in the position to bring them together.

Like Jamie, staring out into that foreboding ocean . . . like Esther, realizing she was risking losing it all . . . like every rescuer who has ever saved someone from a life-or-death situation, there will be fear. That's OK—unless the fear keeps us from going in for the rescue.

We will discuss fear more in chapter 6. One World War II correspondent who covered the Allies' Normandy Invasion on D-Day interviewed many survivors of that brave and brutal assault. They all told about their fear as they neared the beach. And yet they attacked heroically. The correspondent's summary of what he saw: "Courage is not the absence of fear. It is the disregard of it." A spiritual rescuer disregards his fear to give someone he knows a chance to live forever instead of die forever. Your choice about abandoning safety and going in for the rescue is about a dying person's destiny.

God has placed you where you are to save lives. The price for staying on the shore where it's safe is a price too high to pay.

4
GETTING INTO THE LIVES THAT NEED YOU SO MUCH

"DOES HE NOT LEAVE THE NINETY-NINE . . .
AND GO AFTER THE LOST SHEEP UNTIL HE FINDS IT?"
⮞LUKE 15:4⮜

Most of us were still pretty new at this "school thing"—like maybe first grade—when our teacher introduced us to a weekly assignment called "Show and Tell." We had to bring in something from home that we thought would be interesting to the class. The teacher was expecting us to show it to everyone and then explain it to everyone.

You could pretty much count on at least one hamster showing up for Show and Tell. Of course, you could not just give a speech about your personal rodent. "I have this brown, furry, little animal that lives in a cage. He lives in a cage with sawdust in it. His name is Sniffles, and he has bad teeth." No, you could not just tell about your hamster—you had to show him. But neither was it acceptable to Miss Grimley if you just stood in front of the class, held your hamster in your hand for all to see, and said nothing. You could not just show your hamster—you had to tell about it.

God believes in show and tell, particularly when it comes to our communicating the good news about His Son. Because "he has committed to us the message of reconciliation" (2 Corinthians 5:19) and assigned us to be "Christ's ambassadors" (verse 20), there is a lot riding on how well we represent Jesus and deliver His message. The eternity of people you care about depends on their verdict about Jesus, and their verdict may very well hinge on you as the *living proof* of Jesus in their lives.

So you cannot just tell the people around you about Jesus. You have to show them Jesus in ways that will be attractive to them. Most people do not come to believe in Jesus without first believing in a follower of Jesus! When the Master told us to let our light shine before men and women, it was so "they may see your good deeds [show!] and praise your Father in heaven" (Matthew 5:16). Jesus said it would be the way we live that interests people in the relationship that makes us tick.

But just like the first-grade hamster demonstration, you can't just show what you have either—you have to tell about it. The folks around you could watch you for the next fifty years, but they are not ever going to figure out the Gospel that way: "You know, Shirley is such a wonderful person . . . I'll bet Jesus died on the cross for my sins!" That's not going to happen! You have to tell your lost friend about what Jesus did for them. From Resurrection Morning to this very day, the Master's command has been to "go and tell" (Matthew 28:10).

Earlier, I recounted my father-in-law's unforgettable boyhood experience—watching a girl drown in the river—and his determination that "I will never let that happen again." He dedicated himself to learning how to be a rescuer, and in his lifetime he saved four drowning people. If you are beginning to see and feel the "dyingness" Jesus sees in the people you know, then deep inside there will be *a growing determination to learn how to be a spiritual rescuer.*

Recently, as I was having dinner with my friends Roger and Linda, I began to tell them about the writing of this book. Roger, who is very successful in his accounting field, pushed back from the table, turned to his wife, and said, "*This* is the reason God wanted Ron to be here tonight." Unknown to me, God had touched Roger's heart with the lostness of his coworkers and Linda's heart with the eternal peril her neighbors were in. The two were really wanting to know how to be rescuers. The two hours of conversation that followed were so intense that we never even left the dinner table.

That passion to become equipped to save lives is right from the heart of God, who is "not wanting anyone to perish, but everyone to come to repentance" (2 Peter 3:9). In your circle of influence, there is one—probably more than one—who is perishing, a person who is trying to live without the one he or she was made for, who will one day die without hope unless someone points him or her to life. And of all the millions of Jesus-followers on this planet, you may be the one closest to them, the one in the best position to rescue them. And when it comes to a life-or-death emergency, *proximity equals responsibility*. Whoever is on the scene, whoever is in the position to make a difference is responsible.

The tragedy is that so few who are already saved and in God's lifeboat really see, really care about the dying people all around them. Few are willing to step up to their unique, God-given rescue assignment. So multitudes go on dying spiritually, not because they have rejected being rescued, but because no rescuer has ever really made an effort to save them. Using the analogy of harvest urgency, Jesus said, "The harvest [the spiritual readiness of lost people] is plentiful but the workers are few" (Matthew 9:37).

THE "WANT TO" AND THE "HOW TO"

It takes two compelling forces to get us to turn our lifeboat around and begin to bring in as many as we can: the "want to" and the "how to." If you don't care about rescuing the dying, then all the outreach sermons, seminars, and techniques in the world will not move you. One of the greatest mistakes in the church's efforts to reach the lost is assuming that believers have the "want to." We teach Gospel presentations, we plan community outreach programs, we offer excellent training opportunities —and we wonder why so relatively few show up. It may be because we are offering a "how to" for believers who have no "want to." It won't matter how useful the tool is if someone is not interested in doing what the tool does!

On the other hand, a "want to" without a "how to" is destined to fail, too. I remember the day I was supposed to be speaking for an event at the Rosemont Horizon. It is a massive arena near Chicago's O'Hare Airport and surrounded by a "spaghetti bowl" of expressway ramps. My driver was unfamiliar with the roads around the arena, so we spent an exciting few minutes circling the Horizon on one ramp after another.

We just could not seem to find the ramp or the exit that went to the destination we wanted. It wasn't that we couldn't see the auditorium—it is so big that we saw it the whole time, with each ramp giving us a slightly different view. Why weren't we where we were supposed to be? Not because we didn't *want* to be there; we just didn't know *how* to get there!

As God grows in your heart the desire to help the people you know be in heaven with you, your desire to know *how* to effectively communicate Christ will also increase. If you care about spiritually dying people, it is because God has given you "a new heart and put a new spirit in you"; He has removed from you a "heart of stone" and given you a "heart of flesh" (Ezekiel 36:26). Such a heart feels *His* broken heart for the lost, one that is moved by their eternal danger. And you, like my father-in-law after seeing a girl die before his eyes, are ready to know how to be a rescuer.

That means knowing how to both show and tell. It must begin with knowing how to *show* lost people Jesus; that is, after all, how you win the right to *tell* them about Jesus. It will be, in Peter's words, "the hope that you have" that will provide the best opportunities for you to "give an answer to everyone who asks you to give the reason for the hope" (1 Peter 3:15).

REASONS WE AVOID THE RESCUE MISSION

"I don't have the gift." That's one reason people give for not joining Jesus in His rescue mission. And it is true that God gave the gift to be an "evangelist" to only some believers (Ephesians 4:11). But He gave the responsibility for presenting Christ to every believer, gifted or not. Jesus' command to "go into all the world and preach the good news" (Mark 16:15) is for everyone who belongs to Him. He has made all of us believers "Christ's ambassadors, as though God were making his appeal through us" (2 Corinthians 5:20). We can learn from those who have been specially gifted in sharing the Good News, but we cannot delegate the responsibility for our "stretch of the beach" to them.

"I'm not the type." There's another exit through which we can try to escape our lifesaving assignment. Somewhere we may have accepted the misconception that a Christ-ambassador has to be an extrovert, or a good talker, or a salesman-type. The apostle Paul recognized that Apollos and he were "only servants, through whom you came to believe—as the Lord has assigned to each his task" (1 Corinthians 3:5). And God uses different kinds of servants to reach different kinds of people, just as a craftsman uses a wide variety of tools to build what he is building. In His rescue "tool kit," God has some believers who are His forceful "hammers," some who are His rough "sandpaper," some who are His quiet but relentless "screwdrivers," others who are His fine "finishing tools."

Each of us is a special tool in His hands to help lost people "come to believe." The Master Builder will decide when He needs a tool like you for a life He wants to build. You just need to always be ready for Him to use. Bottom line: There is no "right type" for communicating Jesus Christ.

WAYS *ANYONE* CAN COMMUNICATE CHRIST

So no matter what your personality or training or background, you can communicate Christ to the people around you. Here are ten practical ways anyone can communicate Christ. They are an important part of the "how to" of being a spiritual rescuer. We will look at five how-tos in this chapter and complete the list in chapter 6.

These are practical ways you can *show* people Jesus and then *tell* them about Jesus. The first is . . .

LOVE THEM IN THEIR LANGUAGE.

A lost person may resist your invitations to Christian meetings and reject your Christian beliefs, but random acts of love and kindness are usually a bridge into even the hardest hearts. Peter even said that "by doing good you should silence the ignorant talk of foolish men" (1 Peter 2:15). As Jesus carried out His rescue mission on earth, He wrapped His message in concrete acts of love: touching the leper no one would touch, going to dinner with "sinners" the religious avoided, going to a neighborhood where racial barriers said He should never go, cuddling the children who came to Him.

That kind of love tears down walls between a believer and an unbeliever, challenges an unbeliever's misconceptions about Christians being condemning and uncaring, and creates curiosity about what makes this caring person tick.

When we were building our ministry headquarters, an electrical contractor generously donated many of the electrical supplies we needed. One of his employees delivered them by truck. As I talked with him about his boss, the driver said, "I've never worked for a man like him. He really *cares* about his employees." He proceeded to tell me about how his boss had paid for expenses related to a medical emergency in his family. That was this driver's language of love. And this contractor's act of love gave me the opportunity to say, "I know why Bobby would say he's like that. He's just copying his hero—that's Jesus Christ. And he's just loving his employees like Jesus loved him." It was practical love that opened the door to talk naturally about Jesus.

The good news is that *anyone* can show Jesus' love to a lost person. It does not require a theological education or a Hollywood personality. It simply requires that you focus on someone whose eternity you care about and ask yourself this question: "Knowing what I know about this person, what things could I do that would make him or her feel loved?"

The answer may change depending on the person's particular situation, but you might come up with answers like these: babysitting or caring for a live-in parent for free; filling in at work so they can have a day off; helping with a school subject that person is struggling with; providing transportation; offering to do some "dirty work" for them; forgiving a debt; or providing work. You may introduce a newcomer to his new surroundings, open your home for dinner, repair a vehicle or an appliance, take an interest in his special interest or special project, or offer to teach or help the person with something you're naturally good at. Such acts of love are not mere ideas for a list; I have seen them all carried out by real Christians with a real desire to open up someone's life to Jesus' love.

This kind of "rescue loving" involves a conscious effort to identify what would make a lost person feel loved. You can find a person's language of love by asking, "What need does this person have in his/her life right now that I could help with?" You literally go looking for needs into which you can pour the kind of love with which Jesus has loved you. That is part of what it means to "seek and to save" someone who is lost (Luke 19:10).

A second way we can show Jesus to others is to . . .

BE THERE FOR THEM
DURING THE BAD TIMES.

Being there during the bad times is following the Bible command to "mourn with those who mourn" (Romans 12:15b). Again, this is a step of active love that *anyone* can do. When it's hurting time for someone within your reach, you drop everything, realizing this is a precious opportunity to display the Jesus-love you want so much to tell the person about.

People remember who calls or visits when they're sick. They remember who is at the funeral, who comes to the hospital, who pitches in during an emergency. I watched that happen in a major way when the "flood of the century" hit our area in northern New Jersey. The people of our church responded with their hands, feet, and hearts, helping flood victims clean up a filthy mess. They gave clothes and furnishings; they helped in locating alternate housing. There are people in Pequannock and Pompton Plains who know Jesus today because believers who came to their physical rescue opened the door for their spiritual rescue.

When you are thinking about rescuing the spiritually dying, you understand that their moment of crisis is your opportunity to show them Jesus—which means you may have to drop what you're doing to serve as a "be there" person for their storm. When you show up, like Jesus, to serve, you will be in the best possible position to show and tell what Jesus is about.

After the Gulf War in 1991, hundreds of thousands of Kurds had fled Saddam Hussein's Iraq and the persecution they experienced there. They made it to a mountainside just inside the Turkish border where they set up a refugee camp with little or no food, medical help, or sanitation. Christian agencies flooded in with all kinds of emergency supplies, as well as with Gospel literature and sharing of their faith. They felt the urgency of many dying every day.

However, many Christian representatives connected with the Islamic people only from the trucks and distribution points from which they were handing out food and blankets. But missionaries from one agency, Operation Mobilization, really broke through the barriers of another religion with the gospel of Christ. They succeeded in getting close to the people because they were willing to do a job no one wanted to do— pick up the mountains of garbage that were rapidly overtaking the camp. There was a lot of garbage. It was smelly and dirty, and no one wanted to touch it. But the ones who were willing to pick up the garbage were the ones who found many people willing to hear about their Jesus.

Nothing opens doors or hearts like sacrificial acts of love. It is, after all, what Jesus did on the cross. Those who love as He did have the greatest opportunity to tell about His love. When you are there for the bad times of someone you hope to introduce to Jesus, you often find moments of unique spiritual softness—the kind of moments when you can tell the difference Jesus has made for you.

A third way we show Jesus to others is to . . .

BE THERE FOR
THEIR GOOD TIMES.

Being there during the bad times is following the Bible command to "rejoice with those who rejoice" (Romans 12:15a).

It requires no special spiritual giftedness to be at the wedding or to do something special for a birthday, a special event, or an accomplishment. I believe one reason several of our daughter's high school friends ultimately trusted her Savior was the special notes she left in lockers, the creative ways she remembered their birthdays, the big deal she made of their accomplishments. Most people are too wrapped up in their own "small world" to even think about celebrating the good times in the lives of people around them. When a Jesus-follower does "rejoice with those who rejoice," another bridge is built into a life that needs Jesus so much.

A fourth practical way you can show people the love of Jesus is to . .

SHOW REAL
INTEREST IN THEM.

Showing real interest in someone begins by listening to him or her. When someone has lost his train of thought in the middle of a sentence and asked you, "What was I saying?" could you tell the person? Most people are listening too little to each other, distracted by their own thoughts, even thinking of their reply. God tells each of us to be "quick to listen, slow to speak" (James 1:19). If you do that, you will become a standout person in the lives of other people. And by being an active and interested listener, you will win the right to be heard on what really matters to you.

Showing interest is best demonstrated by *asking interested questions.* That's a key way to establish a rescue connection that is within the power of anyone. You may ask about a person or subject they bring up often, the pictures they carry or display, the rock band displayed on a teenager's shirt, anything they are clearly passionate about. This is love in a way that can be felt as well as a way to understand the life of those you want to reach for Jesus. As they come to trust you enough to share some of their life-journey, you may find a natural opportunity to share some of yours, including the difference Jesus has made in that part of your life.

One effort that will make you "salt" and "light" where you are is to be the person who cares enough to *ask the second question.* A flippant "How are you feeling?" or "How ya doin'?" is an almost expected courtesy. No wonder "fine" is often the common answer. But if you really care about a person, there will be times when your radar tells you that there is more to the story than "doin' fine." That is when a second question, spoken in the spirit of caring, can demonstrate genuine personal interest.

My former pastor told about the morning he asked one member how he was doing, got the obligatory "fine," and sensed there was more.

Even though they had started to walk away from each other, my pastor called a second, five-word question back to the man: "Are you really fine, Tom?" The man stopped in his tracks, took the pastor by the arm, and began to pour out a heart full of marital pain. It was the power of that loving second question that opened up a heart. It often does.

A fifth practical way you can show people the love of Jesus is to . . .

PRAY WITH THEM.

Over the years, I have seen unbelievers touched by a promise that believers almost take for granted: "I'll pray for you." If you are working on meaningful relationships with lost people around you—and how are you ever going to reach them if you're not?—then you're going to know when they are struggling. Because you have established yourself as a listening, supportive person in their life, they may very well share with you their concern over a family member, a health issue, a crisis, a hurt, a financial need. Without a doubt, it is time for you to promise that you will talk to God about what they have talked to you about.

But if you are in a situation without other people around, you can ask them if they mind if you start talking to God about it while you're still with them. It is simply a matter of gently asking, "Would you mind if I prayed about it right here, while we're together?" If they decline, just restate your commitment to keep praying about it. I have asked on a number of occasions if I could pray with someone who did not have a relationship with Christ as far as I knew. No one has ever said no. In fact, it is not uncommon to open my eyes at the end of the prayer and see tears in their eyes.

It is quite possible that the person you are praying with has never heard their name mentioned in prayer in their entire life. And by talking to God in their presence, you have actually let that person hear you having your personal relationship with God. It's not just "your beliefs" anymore—it's your relationship. God may even give you a green light to tell what it means to you to be able to go to God like this, and how the wall that separated you from God came down.

After I mentioned this idea to a Christian businessman recently, he said, "That's not really my style, but I need to pray and think about doing it." My experience and the experience of many other believers who have shared with me is that lost people in hurting times are far more ready to be prayed for than we are ready to pray for them. The offer to pray with a friend who does not belong to Christ is virtually a nothing-to-lose deal, even if the individual turns you down. Either way, you have shown you care. Either way, you have demonstrated your personal relationship with God—the relationship you so want your friend or loved one to understand and experience.

GETTING CLOSE ENOUGH TO RESCUE

Rescue always requires involvement in the person's life. Whether it is a toddler trapped in the upper story of a burning house, an earthquake victim in a collapsed apartment—or a person without Christ, facing the death penalty for his or her sin—someone has to get close enough to the person in danger to bring the would-be victim out.

That's why "the Word became flesh and made his dwelling among us" (John 1:14). That's why the Son of God "made himself nothing, taking the very nature of a servant" and "humbled himself and became obedient to death—even death on a cross" (Philippians 2:7–8). And it's why God's ambassador Paul said to people he had helped rescue, "We loved you so much that we were delighted to share with you not only the gospel of God"—telling about Jesus—"but our lives as well"—showing Jesus (1 Thessalonians 2:8).

And this need for the rescuer to get close enough to rescue a person at risk is why it is so important for a spiritual rescuer to build meaningful relationships with spiritually dying people. Not to become like the lost, but to build bridges to the lost—just like our Master. Tragically, those who are already saved tend to spend most of their relationship time with others who are already in the lifeboat. We will be in heaven with those folks forever. But we have only a few years here on earth to help some people outside the lifeboat get to heaven.

It's easy to fill up our lives with other believers. It's comfortable; it's natural. It's hard work to build a relationship with someone outside of Christ, someone with whom we have less and less in common. But *your relationship with a lost person may be the only road that will take that person to the cross.* The lost person probably won't get there by the road marked "church" or "Christian media" or "evangelist." He or she will get to the cross because he or she was *loved there*—by a friend of Jesus who paid the price to become their friend, too.

5
BREAKING
THE
SILENCE

When the clock radio clicks on at wake-up time, my brain doesn't usually kick into high gear immediately. But one morning in college when the radio came on at 6:00 A.M., I distinctly remember being fully conscious within seconds. It was the only time in my life that the news came on and the name of a friend was in the lead story. My sweet dreams were shattered by hearing Cindy's name in the headlines.

As I listened in disbelief, the newscaster recounted how a student at Cindy's university had walked up to the table where she was sitting in the school dining room, pulled out a gun, and shot her in cold blood.

In that awful moment that is forever frozen in my memory, I was plunged into a double shock and a double grief. I was, of course, stunned to think that Cindy, who had always been so alive, was dead. But a deeper, more inconsolable sadness settled over me as I began to think about her eternity. Cindy and I had been really good friends in high school.

We never dated; we just talked with each other a lot. We had talked about so many things: homework, family, sports, the news, the future. I had talked to her about everything—except Jesus. And now all that trivia we had talked about didn't matter at all. And the one thing we hadn't talked about was *all* that mattered for Cindy now.

I don't know if Cindy ever gave her heart to Jesus. All I know is that I never told her about Jesus, and I never got any indication that she knew Him. Even as I think about this tragedy these many years later, it still hurts. Not so much Cindy's death, but my silence.

For a follower of Christ, it is one of life's most haunting regrets—to know that someone you care about has gone into eternity and that you never told that friend about Jesus. I wish we could turn back the clock and have another chance. I know we would not repeat the deadly mistake of failing to let that person know about the Savior who died for them. But we can't go back. What we can do is to ask God's forgiveness for our silence and to turn our regret into determination to tell the people within our reach about Jesus.

The tragedy is that we may spend years around people, talking with them about everything from football to finances to family to friendships—everything but Jesus. Maybe we are so close to them that we can't see what God sees, their eternal lostness without the Savior.

Maybe we have hoped that they would somehow encounter a skilled spiritual "lifeguard" who could better explain the good news about Jesus. We forget that we are the ones who are where they are, in the best position to rescue them. Or maybe our silence comes from believing that somehow our Christian lifestyle will be enough. But while the way we live is the living proof to show them Jesus, they will never understand what Jesus did for them on the cross just by watching us. We will have to *tell them* about Jesus.

In the previous chapter, we began to explore the bridges you can build into lives that need so much, bridges that show Jesus to lost people around us. Those first five ways of communicating Christ are: (1) love them in their language; (2) be there for them during the bad times; (3) be there for their good times; (4) show real interest in them; and (5) pray with them. Such actions are part of *redemptive relationships,* and God uses redemptive relationships to open the hearts of dying people to His life-giving message.

MORE WAYS TO COMMUNICATE CHRIST

The next five ways anyone can communicate Christ help us carry out the second critical phase of our "show and tell" mission from God, to *tell* about Jesus.

The first way to tell about Jesus is . . .

PRAY THE "THREE-OPEN PRAYER."

It's the question every parent faces when it's time for that dreaded talk about those birds and those bees . . . the question every tongue-tied young man faces when he's trying to tell the girl of his dreams that he loves her . . . and the question that every believer who ever wants to tell someone about Christ stumbles over: "How do I *start?*"

In a sense, there are as many answers to that question about sharing Christ as there are people who need to hear about Him; there is a unique, Holy Spirit–directed approach for each individual life. But there are also some steps any believer can take in any situation, under the direction of the Holy Spirit.

The starting point for any rescue conversation about Jesus is *not talking to a person about God but talking to God about that person.* And the "three-open prayer" is a good place to begin. What I call the "three-open prayer" is based on a revealing prayer uttered by perhaps Christ's greatest ambassador, Paul. He issued this call to his friends: "Pray for us, too, that God may open a door for our message, so that we may proclaim the mystery of Christ, for which I am in chains. Pray that I may proclaim it clearly, as I should" (Colossians 4:3–4).

Using this prayer as a launching pad for your own, you can pave the way for eternity-talk by daily believing God for three supernatural preparations. The three-open prayer has three pleas: open the door; open his/her heart; and open my mouth.

"Pray . . . that God may open a door for our message," Paul prayed.

We should first pray . . .

"LORD, OPEN THE DOOR."

An open door is simply a *natural opportunity* to talk about your Jesus-relationship. It will not be very effective to just walk up to unreached people you know and blurt, "Speaking of Jesus . . ." They probably weren't, and they probably aren't planning to. What you need is for the God who opened up the Red Sea for His children to divinely engineer a natural, unforced opportunity for you to introduce Jesus into the conversation. An open door for the good news about Jesus often arises from one of two sources: a common experience or something your lost friend is going through or talking about.

Actually, the world is full of opportunities to talk about spiritual things—for those with eyes to see. So it is important that you also ask the Lord to help you see the opportunity when He puts it in front of you.

A natural opportunity may arise from something that happens in the news. Jesus opened a door for His message when He referred to "those eighteen who died when the tower in Siloam fell on them" (Luke 13:4), an incident apparently from that day's breaking news. A plane crash or the death of someone famous can provide an opportunity for you to tell how it feels to be sure you are ready for your appointment with God—because of Jesus. A headline about an act of anger or violence can open a door to talk about the monster in all of us—and how thankful you are for the animal-taming work of Jesus in your own heart. Events that relate to biblical prophecies about the future can enable you to express the security you have found in knowing the One who will wrap up human history. When a natural disaster hits, there are often people in the news who express the difference their faith is making in their ability to make it through the tragedy. Their testimony gives you a natural opportunity to express how Jesus has been your anchor when everything else was up for grabs.

An alert spiritual rescuer has two regular "homework" assignments:

(1) through broadcast journalism, the newspaper, and news magazines, know what is going on in the news; and (2) as you absorb the day's news, ask God to give you His perspective on what's happening and a way to relate it to your relationship with Him.

A natural opportunity may develop from something that is happening in your family or in their family. If you are a parent, many times you have faced situations with a child where you've thought, "I couldn't do it without Jesus." If the person you want to know Jesus is a parent, then your parental struggles or theirs can provide a natural way for you to say how Jesus can affect "mommying" or "daddying." Conversations that turn to marital issues or relationships with parents or family tragedies can also open doors for explaining the "Jesus difference."

God also uses *our hurting times* to provide opportunities to naturally bring up Jesus. Although Karen's dad had already been through several life-threatening medical crises, he was not even sick the day God took him; he was only in the hospital to assess the damage from a fall. But three times that day he told my wife, "I just want to go home and be with Jesus." He had just completed a routine admitting interview when he suddenly and quietly slipped away—with Karen the only one in the room with him.

In moments, eight nurses had rushed into the room, shocked that this man had died so suddenly and unexpectedly. He had just told them he did not want resuscitation if that were ever an option—so the nurses' concern quickly focused on this woman who had just watched her father slip away. But God gave my wife some "amazing grace" in that tender moment; she ended up comforting the nurses instead of them comforting her! She said, "My daddy is home with Jesus. He was ready to go." And then, right in that hospital room that was suddenly full of eternity, she prayed with those nurses, reviewing the good news about Jesus as she prayed.

In many conversations during the days that followed, Karen had natural opportunities to explain how Jesus makes us ready to die and ready to deal with death. Hearts were open in that especially tender time, and my wife knew that many of her prayers for "open doors" were being answered by this difficult moment in her life. Years ago, when I nearly lost Karen to a serious illness, I had no idea how God would use that awful time to give me open doors to talk about Jesus—the one relationship I can never, never lose.

Strangely, it is often our hurting times that provide our best times to communicate Christ. The beating, unjust suffering, and imprisonment Paul and Silas experienced provided an unusual platform for them to point people to Jesus. Right in that Philippian jail, "about midnight, Paul and Silas were praying and singing hymns to God, and the other prisoners were listening to them" (Acts 16:25). All eyes, all ears are on you when you are in a hurting time; it is a powerful time for people to see and hear about your Jesus.

The second supernatural preparation you can ask God for in your three-open prayer for the spiritual rescue of someone you know is . . .

"LORD, OPEN HIS/HER HEART."

When God is opening a door for you to tell about Jesus, He is also preparing the heart of a lost person to hear it. The Bible says of Lydia, the first person to come to Christ in Europe, "The Lord opened her heart to respond to Paul's message" (Acts 16:14). That is a miracle the Lord has repeated countless times for countless Christians in countless rescue moments.

And this heart-opening work of God plays an important part in a spiritual rescue. Remember that God is the One who prepares the hearts of the needy. As you are praying for open doors, it is important, too, that you pray for open hearts in the people you want in heaven with you. God has many ways of answering that prayer, bringing events, other people, and experiences into their lives that make them surprisingly ready for someone who does what Jesus does. In fact, when Jesus said that "the harvest is plentiful" (Matthew 9:37), He must have been thinking about readiness. Usually, when I ask a farmer, the first word he thinks of when I say "harvest" is "ready." Much more than we can tell from the impression people give us, the "ready" in many hearts is plentiful, especially when we have spent time in God's presence, asking and believing Him for someone's heart to be opened by Him.

An open door provides the opportunity to tell about Jesus. An open heart creates an environment in which the Good News will sound like good news. The third request in the three-open prayer generates the courage and the words it takes to deliver the life-saving message:

"LORD, OPEN MY MOUTH."

"Pray that I may proclaim [the gospel of Christ] clearly, as I should" (Colossians 4:4). Thus the third supernatural preparation you can ask God for is "Lord, when You open the door, help me see the opportunity and help me open my mouth to talk about Jesus in an appropriate way."

If you find yourself feeling "chicken" when spiritual opportunities come, join the club! After more than thirty years of presenting Christ, I still sometimes find myself in the Chicken Club, struggling to find the courage to say what I know God wants me to say about Jesus. It helps me some to know who one of the charter members of the Chicken Club was—no one less than the great apostle Paul.

Paul was a veteran Christ-communicator when he wrote these words: "When I came to you, brothers, I did not come with eloquence or superior wisdom. . . . I came to you in weakness and fear, and with much trembling" (1 Corinthians 2:1, 3). This great preacher of the Gospel still got scared when it was time to talk about Jesus. But he went on to explain why our sense of fear and inadequacy can be a good thing. "My message and my preaching were not with wise and persuasive words, but with *a demonstration of the Spirit's power,* so that your faith might not rest on men's wisdom, but on *God's power*" (1 Corinthians 2:4–5, italics added).

In other words, when we're scared, we get out of the way and let God take over. And when there isn't much of you, there's a whole lot of God! And that rescue conversation becomes much more than a human exchange. It becomes a supernatural transaction in which something from God's heart passes through a heart like yours and right into the heart of a lost and dying person!

Paul's prayer for an "open mouth" goes beyond just a cry for courage. He dares to ask for the actual words to use in presenting Christ. It's a prayer that should become a regular part of the life of any spiritual rescuer. "Pray also for me, that whenever I open my mouth, words may be given me so that I will fearlessly make known the mystery of the gospel. . . . Pray that I may declare it fearlessly, as I should" (Ephesians 6:19–20). God is waiting to give you what you don't have: the courage to speak and the words to speak, available upon request.

God will open the door . . . God will open their heart . . . God will open your mouth—in answer to your fervent, faithful prayer.

In addition to praying the three-open prayer, there is a second way to tell people about Jesus:

WRITE A THANK-YOU LETTER TO THEM.

Few people ever write one or even remember to say "thank you." That is why a thank-you letter can be a very positive way for you to communicate Christ to someone you care about. When you write your feelings, you tend to say it better (for one thing, no one is interrupting or challenging what you're saying!), and the person reading it tends to receive it better and remember it longer.

No doubt, there are people in your world, including family members, friends, and coworkers, who deserve some thanks from you. Your written appreciation could provide a wonderful context in which to include your desire for them to experience the love and peace of Jesus Christ.

You can begin by telling that person specific things you appreciate about him or her. First, tell the person things he is; for instance, generous, encouraging, steady, honest, challenging, hardworking, loving, patient. Then mention things the person has done; for instance, provided for you, made you think, accepted you, comforted you, taken time for you, provided opportunities for you, or believed in you.

In a situation where your parents may feel you have, by following Christ, abandoned the religious tradition they raised you in, it is important to thank them for starting you in the right direction. So often, the impression a reborn believer gives—or the impression the uncommitted family member draws—is that the son or daughter's commitment to Christ is a total departure from the way he or she was raised. On the contrary, parents should be thanked for whatever spiritual training or background they gave. For instance, you can say, "I appreciate the way you made sure I got to church" or "I appreciate that you told me about the Bible" or "I appreciate that you made sure I knew God was important."

Most parents gave some nudging toward at least a belief in God. By affirming that, a son or daughter can go on to say, "And I kept going down that road you started me on, and I'm so glad I did. That's where I discovered who Jesus is, how much He loves us, and how He can change our lives."

Whatever your relationship with the person you are writing to, your sincere and specific gratitude can open a heart and build a bridge into that heart. In that context of appreciation, you can tell the person about your personal love relationship with Jesus Christ and your desire to be sure he share that relationship with you—because that person means so much to you. When you love someone and you've tasted something good, you just naturally want the other to taste it, too! You may have found a booklet or pamphlet that effectively presents the Good News; if the Spirit seems to give you the green light, include that presentation as "something that helped me understand how a relationship with Jesus works."

When you present a relationship with Jesus in the context of your heartfelt thanks, you are doing it just like the Bible says to do it, "with gentleness and respect" (1 Peter 3:15) and with "conversation" that is "always full of grace" (Colossians 4:6).

Another way to tell people about Jesus is to . . .

PREPARE YOUR "TESTIMONY TOOL KIT."

The businessman next to me on the airplane responded in great detail when I asked him about his burgeoning computer business. He told me about his company's explosive growth, his relentless travel schedule, and his growing staff. After listening for much of the flight, I slipped in a question that quickly changed the tone and direction of the conversation, "Do you have any children?" My neighbor turned suddenly subdued as he answered, "Yes. I have a son." Having talked about the challenges of business, I mentioned how much more challenging it is to be a dad. He completely agreed and expressed some of his struggle of fathering to me.

If I was going to bring up Jesus in the few remaining minutes of our flight, it clearly needed to be a daddy's Savior. So I began to share with my neighbor the pressures I felt as a father, the way that parenting revealed hurtful traits in me that I was powerless to change—and how Jesus was enlarging me to be the kind of dad my children needed. The dad connection (my "clever disguise" at that moment) allowed me to share how sin, the "disease of *me*," is what eats away at our closest relationships. I also explained how Jesus' actions on the cross means that I can change.

My neighbor listened responsively, partly because I had listened to him, partly because we were talking about a need he felt, and partly because my testimony was customized to his situation. It is these kinds of *customized testimonies*—part of what I call the "testimony tool kit"—that we need so we are "prepared to give an answer to everyone who asks you to give the reason for the hope that you have" (1 Peter 3:15).

Personal testimonies are powerful vehicles for telling about Jesus. They have been around since the days of that blind man Jesus healed testifying that "one thing I do know. I was blind but now I see!" (John 9:25). The spiritually dying people you know aren't particularly interested in the beliefs you believe or the religion you're a part of. They are a lot more likely to be interested in the Person who miraculously changed your life. But not just one part of your life . . . not just the spiritual part of your life.

You cannot be around church for long without hearing people talk about their "testimony," and what that usually means is the story of how their relationship with Jesus Christ began. But that is only part of their testimony, only one chapter in their personal Jesus-story. (In a future chapter, we will explore how to think through and tell this "story only you can tell.")

As you prepare yourself for rescue opportunities, one helpful step is to think through your "testimony tool kit," developing different approaches to introducing Jesus for different people. Clearly, your story of what Jesus did on the cross is the same every time. It is only your *approach,* your *package* that changes. That is part of what Ambassador Paul had in mind when he said, "To the Jews I became like a Jew, to win the Jews. To those under the law I became like one under the law . . . so as to win those under the law. To those not having the law I became like one not having the law . . . so as to win those not having the law. To the weak I became weak, to win the weak." And then Paul summarized his overriding approach: "I have become all things to all men so that by all possible means I might save some" (1 Corinthians 9:20–22).

To prepare your "testimony tool kit" for communicating in different kinds of situations, you can think through questions such as: How has my relationship with Jesus and what He did on the cross made a difference in . . .

- my lonely times?
- my depressing times?
- the kind of marriage partner I am?
- my living single?
- the kind of parent I am?
- my stressed-out times?
- my times of pain or loss?

Those are some of the chapters in your Jesus-story. Depending on what issues may come up in a conversation, you can read from the "chapter" of your life that connects with the person you're with. No matter where each chapter starts, be sure that it ends at the cross of Jesus. That is where every Christian testimony ultimately points. With a tool kit of personal testimonies in your heart, many everyday conversations can become natural opportunities to bring up Jesus.

The next way to tell people about Jesus is to . . .

LEND THE PERSON SOMETHING CHRISTIAN.

Since everyday believers are Jesus' best representatives, then there need to be ways to communicate Christ that anybody can do. And lending a Christian resource to a person without Christ certainly requires no special gifts or training. What you lend may be a book, an audio cassette, a CD, or a video that addresses a need or issue that person cares about and clearly presents a relationship with Christ in the process.

When Jesus was describing our part in the miracle process of someone turning to Him, He spoke in agricultural terms: "This is what the kingdom of God is like. A man scatters seed on the ground" (Mark 4:26). What followed is a supernatural process that ends in spiritual harvest, according to Christ. But it begins with a spiritual "farmer" scattering some seed. That is what you're doing when you prayerfully lend a Gospel-presenting resource to a lost friend or loved one.

Why lend it instead of giving it? Because you want that person to give it back so you can ask what they thought about what they read or heard. Pray for a natural opportunity to share how that message has changed your life. It is probably best to let the "lendee" know a time that you need to have it back. If they have forever to get to it, it will probably take forever.

The next way to tell people about Jesus is to . . .

INVITE THE PERSON TO AN OUTREACH EVENT.

Every year our church has presented an impressive Christmas music cantata. Since Christmas is the time of the year when it is more natural to think and talk about Jesus than any other, it can be prime time for some natural rescue opportunities. One thing that has meant for Karen and me is *bringing* to the Christmas cantata, not just *coming* to it.

We had special friends we wanted to bring, and we learned a simple but important step that takes an invitation to another whole level: Make it an event where you do something special together either before or after the outreach event. For us, that meant a special dinner one year.

Then we realized that coming back for dessert was a better idea because it gave us an opportunity to talk about what we had all heard—and to share how the Baby of Bethlehem had changed everything.

As a spiritual rescuer, it is important to be alert for events that might be on the "wavelength" of a lost person you care about. It could be sports, concerts, a seminar, or something their children are involved with. As always, seek the leading of the Holy Spirit as to whether this opportunity is from Him, for the preparation of your friend's heart, and for a natural opportunity for you to communicate your Jesus as a result of this outreach. None of us Jesus-ambassadors can delegate our responsibility to a speaker or musician at an event. The real issue is trusting God to use the outreach to launch a supernaturally natural opportunity to tell about your Savior.

THE DEADLY SIN OF SILENCE

About 1200 B.C., the people of Samaria were starving. The Jews' Aramean enemies had besieged the city, and it was becoming increasingly impossible to find anything to eat. They were so desperate they would do *anything* for some food. They were offering to pay any price for a little food. Some were even turning to cannibalism.

But if conditions were bad for those inside the city, they were virtually hopeless for the lepers who were forced to live just outside the city. They depended on the scraps and handouts of the people in Samaria—who, of course, had no scraps.

The Bible reports in 2 Kings 7 that as four lepers stared starvation in the face, they evaluated their options and decided they were all bad ones. They concluded: "'Why stay here until we die? If we say, "We'll go into the city"—the famine is there, and we will die. And if we stay here, we will die. So let's go over to the camp of the Arameans and surrender. If they spare us, we live; if they kill us, then we die'" (2 Kings 7:3–4). The four lepers made their way toward the sprawling enemy camp. They arrived to find it empty. The Lord had created "the sound of a great army," and just that frightening sound made the Arameans flee for their lives, thinking they were under attack by Israel's allies. (See 2 Kings 7:5–7.)

The stunned lepers soon enjoyed their bounty. "They ate and drank, and carried away silver, gold and clothes, and went off and hid them" (verse 8). But they forgot the needs of those starving in Samaria. They were totally occupied with consuming the blessings of the Lord's victory. Meanwhile mothers in the city nearby were watching their sons and daughters starve to death.

Finally, the men heard a wake-up call in their heart. "'We're not doing right. This is a day of good news and we are keeping it to ourselves. . . . Let's go at once and report this'" (verse 9). What the four men said to each other is a sobering wake-up call to all of us who are consuming the blessings of the Lord's victory on the cross.

"We are keeping it to ourselves . . . we're not doing right." Those words cut right to my heart. How often have I—how often have all of us—kept the good news about Jesus to ourselves, especially when we know that we are surrounded by people who are spiritually starving to death? Like those lepers in the story, we have been rescued by a gracious God and then led to the soul-satisfying banquet Jesus made possible. We are surrounded by His blessings now. But it was never meant to stop with us.

And that is why your heart may be restless. Because God is stirring your soul to "go at once and report this" wonderful news of His love to people who will die if you don't. He rescued you *so you could be a rescuer.*

You've been silent about Jesus too many times. But, by God's grace, you'll be silent no more.

6
WOULD YOU LIKE TO SUPER-SIZE THAT?

"THIS IS WHAT THE LORD SAYS TO YOU:
'DO NOT BE AFRAID OR DISCOURAGED. . . .
FOR THE BATTLE IS NOT YOURS, BUT GOD'S.'"
◆2 CHRONICLES 20:15◆

America's fast-food restaurants have found another way to make your wallet a little lighter and theirs a little heavier. You place your order for, let's say, a Big Chomper, fries, and a drink. You've reviewed the options (even though you have the menu memorized) and made the big decision. But then the girl throws out that question: "Would you like to super-size that?"

Depending on the restaurant, it could be "biggie-size" or "jumbo-size," but the idea is the same. And because so many Americans have answered yes, many Americans are now "super-sized"!

A super-sized order may be what it takes to satisfy some people's large appetite. Not just at a fast-food restaurant, but also in pursuing a life that will make a greater spiritual difference. Many of us have a deep restlessness in our souls, a growing appetite for a Christian experience that is more fulfilling, more challenging than what we have now.

This persistent sense that there must be "something more" is what opens our hearts to a bold new touch of God on our lives . . . and to the life-enlarging realization that Jesus is calling us to join Him in His eternal mission of rescuing spiritually dying people. We begin to see that He has uniquely positioned us to help some people we know be in heaven with us. There is no greater significance your life could have than that! This is the call to greatness—to be consumed by the greatest cause on the planet, the cause for which the Son of God gave His life . . .

"TO SEEK AND SAVE WHAT WAS LOST" (LUKE 19:10).

So as God listens to your "order" for what you would like Him to do in your life, I can imagine Him asking: "Would you like Me to super-size that?" He is, after all, the God "who is able to do immeasurably more than all we ask or imagine, according to his power that is at work within us" (Ephesians 3:20). He is waiting for us to pursue that "immeasurably more," His call to greatness. Our hearts will never be satisfied until we do.

As God begins to move your heart to care about spiritually dying people—to be, as He is, "not wanting anyone to perish" (2 Peter 3:9)— you quickly become aware of your own inadequacy. As you develop Jesus' eyes to see the "dyingness" of the people around you and your responsibility to do something about it, a lot of paralyzing fears start to rear their heads. "What will they think of me?" "What if I mess it up?" "How am I going to approach them?" The key words in all our "yeah buts" and "what ifs" are *I* and *me*.

And that's the problem. Many Jesus-followers miss their destiny on earth because they are so focused on themselves. They focus on themselves because they underestimate and undertrust God. The result is that they underpray. And prayer is the weapon that unleashes all the power of God to bring dying people to the cross of Jesus.

That is why Paul, God's great ambassador, was constantly asking his friends to pray for him in his spiritual rescue work. He said: "Join me in my struggle by praying to God for me" (Romans 15:30); "Pray also for me, that . . . words may be given me. . . . Pray that I may declare it fearlessly" (Ephesians 6:19–20); "Pray for us, too, that God may open a door for our message. . . . Pray that I may proclaim it clearly" (Colossians 4:3–4); "Pray for us that the message of the Lord may spread rapidly" (2 Thessalonians 3:1); and simply, "Brothers, pray for us" (1 Thessalonians 5:25).

This business of communicating Christ to lost people is supernatural stuff! It isn't about your compelling persuasiveness, your clever approach, your winning personality, or your verbal ability. It's about God working in a lost person's heart and through you to change someone's eternal address. "It is God who works in you to will and to act according to his good purpose" (Philippians 2:13). And since it is God, prayer becomes your most powerful tool in reaching into the heart of someone who is away from Jesus. In fact . . .

PRAYER IS THE PRIMARY METHOD OF GETTING SOMEONE YOU CARE ABOUT TO JESUS.

So, knowing how to talk to God about lost people is at least as critical as knowing how to talk to lost people about God. Once we understand how to unleash the super-sizing power of God through prayer, we are ready to make a greater difference than we ever dreamed we could.

A PRAYER, A FACE, AND A MIRACLE

Susan couldn't wait to tell me. She cornered me right after the Christian leaders' breakfast at which I had just spoken. Susan had attended a "prayer concert" for the lost that I had led two days before. Both the leaders' breakfast and the prayer concert were helping to lay the spiritual groundwork for an upcoming evangelism mobilization we call Make a Difference Week. After the believers there broke into groups of threes, forming prayer triplets, I suggested they ask God for one person to pray for who did not belong to Jesus, as far as they knew.

Susan told me that as she prayed in her triplet, it was if God showed her the face of her coworker Grant. Although she knew Grant seemed anything but a likely candidate to receive the Gospel, he was the one she prayed for by name that night.

The very next day at work, Grant began talking to Susan about a subject that had come up often in recent weeks: how much money was coming his way recently. Much to her surprise, Susan began to tell her coworker about "a man Jesus told about who was getting richer and richer, so much so that he was running out of places to put everything he was accumulating. Then one day God spoke to him and said, 'You're going to die this very night and I will require your soul of you.' "

Grant was visibly shaken by what he heard. In fact, he left the room. When he didn't come back right away, Susan felt compelled to go after him. And when she asked how he was doing, he blurted, "I've got so much garbage in my life." Susan tried to conceal her amazement as Grant began to pour out his heart about a list of sins he was ashamed of. Susan knew it was time to tell him about the forgiveness Jesus offers because He died to pay for every one of those sins.

Susan almost exploded as she told me, "And he gave his heart to Christ right *there*—at *work!*" She traced that miracle right back to a season of prayer the night before when she had obeyed the Spirit and interceded for Grant by name. My guess is that Susan now has a list of unreached friends and associates she is claiming for Christ in prayer.

Of course, the answers do not often come that quickly. But every rebirth miracle is nothing less than an act of God, usually in answer to the rescue praying of one of His children. Susan's miracle vividly demonstrates the lordship of Christ in every step of our efforts to rescue the dying. It was God who planted a burden for a specific lost person in her heart. He provided a natural opportunity to bring up Jesus, prepared her coworker's heart, gave Susan the words and approach to use, and drew her friend to the Savior.

SPIRITUAL LIFESAVING: IT'S A GOD-THING

In order for us to make an eternal impact on anyone, we have to understand what a total "God-thing" the saving of a soul really is. Grant's coming to Christ—*anyone's* coming to Christ—has its roots long ago in eternity where "he chose us in him before the creation of the world"... where God "predestined us to be adopted as his sons through Jesus Christ" (Ephesians 1:4–5). It is all part of that awesome process in which "those God foreknew he also predestined to be conformed to the likeness of his Son" (Romans 8:29).While theologians may debate how the sovereignty of God and the free will of man come together in God's saving work, it is clear that *God has had His eye on us since before there was a world.*

It is also clear that the same apostle Paul who wrote the most profound biblical passages on the total sovereignty of God in rescuing people is the same man whose message was "Believe in the Lord Jesus, and you will be saved" (Acts 16:31). He is the same man who said so passionately, "We implore you on Christ's behalf: Be reconciled to God" (2 Corinthians 5:20). Paul prayed as if it was all up to God and worked as if it was all up to him! Similarly, this God who "foreknew" and "predestined" and "chose" is also the God who calls those already rescued to "go into all the world and preach the good news to all creation" (Mark 16:15).

As we struggle with the personal insecurities that so often keep us from sharing Jesus' life-giving message, it is liberating to realize how very much is up to God and how relatively little is up to us. It is our responsibility to present the good news about Jesus; it is not our responsibility to persuade a person to choose Christ. Jesus made it clear that it is the Holy Spirit who "will convict the word of guilt in regard to sin and righteousness and judgment" (John 16:8). Jesus let us know that "no one can come to me unless the Father who sent me draws him" (John 6:44). It is something beyond the reach of any human being to get someone to Jesus.Without the Father's drawing, no one could or would come to the Son. It is such a relief to know that you are the presenter; God is the Persuader.

Jesus provided a visual image of the invisible processes of a sinner coming into God-relationship when He described it in terms of a farmer harvesting his crops. (See Matthew 9:38.) Later, Paul summarized God's role and our role, writing, "I planted the seed, Apollos watered it, but God made it grow. So neither he who plants nor he who waters is anything, but only God, who makes things grow" (1 Corinthians 3:6–7). The Lord expects us to plant the seed of the Gospel in lost hearts; but the results, just as in farming or gardening, are in God's hands.

Since the rescue of people we know is such a "God-thing," the role of praying to God about it cannot be understated. Our prayer for dying people and for us as His rescuers is the foundation for our whole life-or-death mission. We join Jesus in His rescue mission first on our knees.

Amy Carmichael, the heroic pioneer missionary to India, understood what that meant. She felt called by God to help rescue girls, and later boys, from being used and abused in the temples of India. Few missionaries or even Indian Christians supported her. But she wrote: "Sometimes it was as if I saw the Lord Jesus Christ kneeling alone, as He knelt long ago under the olive trees. The trees were tamarind now, the tamarinds that I see as I look up from this writing. And the only thing that one who cared could do was to go softly and kneel down beside Him so that He would not be alone in His sorrow over the little children."[1]

Going softly and kneeling down beside Jesus to join Him in His passionate praying for the lost ones—that is ground zero for making an eternal difference. Knowing *how* to pray for the lost becomes "Basic Training" for a spiritual rescuer.

BULLIES, BUTTERFLIES, AND A BIG FATHER

I suppose every neighborhood has its bully. Ours did. His name was Boomer. For all the children on our block in Chicago, Boomer was our own personal terrorist—intimidating us, stealing our stuff, beating us up if we looked at him the wrong way. But the day he took my precious White Sox cap was the last straw. Even though I was just a little guy, I marched down the street and walked to where no child ever dared to go, right to Boomer's back porch. I knocked on the door and dared to ask for my stuff back.

"You were a brave little guy!" you might say. Not really. There is one small fact I haven't told you yet: My *father* went with me. And that made all the difference. Boomer was bigger than I was—but my father was bigger than Boomer.

As we think about stepping up to being God's rescuer for the people we know, there are so many fears and insecurities that try to bully us into silence. We know we ought to do it; we know this is life or death for someone we care about. But somehow our fears of their reaction or our failure loom as big as Boomer did to me and my friends. What sets us free to tell someone about Jesus is the realization that . . .

OUR FATHER IS GOING WITH US. HE IS THE ONE WHO WILL MAKE THE DIFFERENCE.

When you realize how much of this rescue mission is God and how little of it is you, you can dare to do and say what you would never otherwise be able to.

After thirty years of presenting Christ to people, the apostle Paul was still scared. (See again 1 Corinthians 2:3.) I can relate to that. As often and as long as I have been telling people about Jesus, I still feel major butterflies when I know I'm with someone who needs to hear about Jesus from me. Years of experience do not remove the intimidation factor of opening your mouth for Christ. But such fear can be a very good thing.

Paul said that because he was afraid, "My message and my preaching were not with wise and persuasive words, but with a demonstration of the Spirit's power, so that your faith might not rest on men's wisdom, but on God's power" (1 Corinthians 2:4–5). Your feelings of fear and inadequacy can drive you to retreat—or they can drive you to depend totally on God. Your "I can't, Lord, but You can" transforms a human process into something supernatural. And suddenly there are words and power and results that you cannot explain. If your fear focuses you on yourself, you will retreat into silence. But if your fear focuses you on what God can do, you will move beyond yourself and allow God's lifesaving message to come out of your mouth.

You do not start praying for lost people you can reach when you are suddenly in the middle of an opportunity to speak for Him. To be an effective spiritual rescuer, you need to make praying for dying people part of your life. As you pray regularly for things only God can do, you remind yourself of who is really in charge here, and your confidence grows. Remember, your times of praying for the lost and for your rescue responsibility are ground zero for the great work God is giving you to do.

So often we are trusting in the "powerless P's" to get people to Jesus: persuasion, programs, promotion, and personality. But this is a God-thing from beginning to end. So our prayer efforts on behalf of people without Jesus are the deciding factor.

RESCUE PRAYING

It's a sunny winter afternoon, and a board is lying on the ground. Even though the sun has been shining all day, the board does not even get warm. But, as many of us learned as children, something amazing happens when you hold a piece of magnifying glass between the sun and a spot on that board. After a while, the wood under the glass starts to feel warm . . . then hot. Ultimately, you might even be able to ignite a little fire.

It's the same sun and the same board. What's the difference? Focused energy. When you focus the power of the sun on one particular spot, the sun changes that spot. And when you focus the power of God on a particular person or need, the power of God changes what you focus it on. Powerful praying is focused praying.

When it comes to praying for the spiritual rescue of dying people, the Bible helps us to know some specific targets on which to focus our praying. As you unleash the power of God on the rescue mission around you, there are at least five targets for rescue praying. First . . .

PRAY FOR
NATURAL OPPORTUNITIES.

Paul modeled this when he asked his friends to pray that "God may open a door for our message, so that we may proclaim the mystery of Christ" (Colossians 4:3). When you pray this way, you are asking God to put you in situations and conversations where it will be natural for you to bring up Jesus. Thus, when Susan prayed for her coworker Grant, God created a natural opportunity for her to talk about Jesus as Grant talked about the money he was accumulating. When you are praying for open doors to present life's most important relationship, you don't even have to pray, "Lord, if it's Your will." It is!

Second, during rescue praying . . .

PRAY FOR
PREPARED HEARTS.

If God were a doctor, I think He would be a heart specialist. He is so skillful at softening hearts, changing hearts, preparing hearts to receive a message from Him. As Paul met the woman who would become the first European he would lead to Christ, "the Lord opened her heart to respond to Paul's message" (Acts 16:14). And there is no heart beyond His reach.

Ezra records that the Lord filled the hearts of His people with joy "by changing the attitude of the king" and that the Lord had "put it into the king's heart to bring honor to the house of the Lord" (Ezra 6:22, 7:27). In fact, "the king's heart is in the hand of the Lord; he directs it like a watercourse wherever he pleases" (Proverbs 21:1).

So praying for God to "open a heart," "change an attitude," or "put it into their hearts" is praying for something God loves to do. It is important to pray for a lost person's heart to be ready because, as Jesus taught us, the condition of the ground determines what happens to the seed (Matthew 13:3–8).

Third, during rescue praying . . .

PRAY FOR YOUR HEART.

It is not natural for you to care deeply about lost people around you; it is *supernatural*. That is why it is critical that you regularly ask Jesus to give you His heart for the people you know and meet; to give you His eyes to be able to see them as the dying people outside the lifeboat.

Matthew recorded that "when [Jesus] saw the crowds, he had compassion on them, because they were harassed and helpless, like sheep without a shepherd" (Matthew 9:36). But apparently most of His followers didn't see what He saw. Otherwise, there would not have been the tragedy Jesus described when He declared, "the harvest is plentiful but the workers are few" (Matthew 9:37). People are dying spiritually, not because they're not ready for the Good News, but because God's people aren't ready to go bring them in.

That is why Jesus says, "Ask the Lord of the harvest, therefore, to send out workers into his harvest field" (Matthew 9:38). Without regular prayer to have Jesus' broken heart for the lost, our hearts will grow cold and self-absorbed again. When you ask God for a heart that continues to see the desperation and "dyingness" of the people around you, you are enlisting again in the greatest cause you can live for.

Fourth, during rescue praying . . .

PRAY FOR GOD'S WORDS.

My friend Ian has a serious stutter—except when he gets in front of a crowd. Suddenly, his speech is flawless. In fact, Ian is one of the most respected, sought-after Christian communicators in his country. Something supernatural happens when Ian *has* to speak well. What God does for my friend, He wants to do for you when it's time for you to speak for Jesus. He offers a divine takeover that will carry you beyond your limitations. That is what Paul was counting on when he asked his friends to "pray . . . that whenever I open my mouth, words may be given me so that I will fearlessly make known . . . the gospel" (Ephesians 6:19).

God has positioned you to be His rescuer in the circle of people you know. And you may say, "I don't know what to say. I can't do it." You're right. You can't—but *He* can. God will take you outside yourself to make you His messenger delivering *His* words. He wants to display His power by giving you words and wisdom you don't even know you have. Pray for God to do that kind of miracle for you whenever you have opportunity to tell someone about His Son.

Fifth, during rescue praying . . .

PRAY FOR
A PARALYZED ENEMY.

Every person without Christ is a prisoner needing to be "rescued . . . from the dominion of darkness and brought . . . into the kingdom of the Son he loves" (Colossians 1:13). And Satan has no intention of giving up his prisoner without a fight. Jesus said, "How can anyone enter a strong man's house and carry off his possessions unless he first ties up the strong man? [Only] then he can rob his house" (Matthew 12:29). The devil is that strong man and people without the Savior are his "possessions."

Recently, I talked with a friend who is a retired policeman, and he helped me see a new perspective on this "first tying up the strong man." Frank was telling me about the training police officers receive in how to handle a hostage situation when someone is holed up in a building, holding innocent hostages he has no plans to release. My friend told me that police rescue strategy begins by cutting off all outside connections to the building. There is no more heat, phone, water, electricity, or any provisions of food. In Frank's words, "Never let the hostage taker be in control." If less risky measures are not effective, the police may then resort to an agent like tear gas that will immobilize the captor.

It is this step of removing Satan's control and immobilizing him that is often forgotten in spiritual rescue efforts. We just go charging in to try to bring out one of his hostages, only to emerge without the hostage and perhaps wounded ourselves. We forgot to "tie up the strong man" before we try to rescue a prisoner he has held for a long time.

But we have no power to immobilize the enemy. That takes Someone stronger. Jesus said, "When a strong man, fully armed, guards his own house, his possessions are safe." (Remember, those "possessions" are people you know!) "But when someone stronger attacks and overpowers him, he takes away the armor in which the man trusted and divides up the spoils" (Luke 11:21–22). So our job is to unleash the power of Jesus—that "Someone stronger"—through prayer, against the enemy. When Jesus takes away control from the hostage taker, we can go in and, in His strength, bring out the hostages. The battle is won on our knees.

PRAYED HOME

Your time praying for those outside the lifeboat and for you as you reach out to them is the deciding factor in the outcome. "The prayer of a righteous man is powerful and effective" (James 5:16). Hudson Taylor, the pioneer missionary to China, stressed, "How important to learn to move man, through God, by prayer alone." And D. L. Moody, who was instrumental in more people coming to Christ than any man in the nineteenth century, said, "Every great movement of God can be traced to a kneeling figure."[2]

As you talk with God about your rescue mission—for natural opportunities, for prepared hearts and your heart, for God's words and a paralyzed enemy—you will be diving into the redemptive river of God, and "where the river flows everything will live" (Ezekiel 47:9). You are entering into an eternal lifesaving process that stretches from eternity past, through the death and resurrection of Jesus, to someone in your world whom He died for, and into that person's eternity. And as you bathe the entire process in prayer, your fears begin to diminish and your confidence and courage begin to grow, "for *the Lord* will be your confidence" (Proverbs 3:26, italics added).

Without one woman's rescue praying, my precious wife Karen would not even be here today. Her grandfather, Bill Hadley, was an alcoholic from the age of twelve. He spent time in jail after jail, prison after prison, so enslaved that he would dig the gold fillings out of his teeth to get money to buy cocaine. Bill Hadley was, by any human reckoning, a spiritual "Mission Impossible."

One night this shell of a man decided that life was no longer worth living. He made his way down South State Street in Chicago toward Lake Michigan where he planned to end it all. But that's when the miracle happened. As he walked to what he thought would be his death, Bill Hadley found life. He heard a familiar song coming from inside Pacific Garden Mission, a song his Christian mother had taught him. He felt compelled to go in. A personal worker saw him and shared the love and forgiveness of Jesus with him.

That night, Bill opened his heart to the Savior and was, as he would often say in years to come, "not reformed, but *transformed.*" My wife's grandfather never had a taste for alcohol or drugs from that night on; he was truly a "new creation" in Christ (2 Corinthians 5:17). In fact, Bill Hadley married a beautiful Christian woman, fathered a baby girl who would grow up to be my wife's mother, and launched a cross-country evangelistic ministry in his "Little Church on Wheels." He became a passionate messenger of the transforming power of a living Christ.

But the battle for Bill Hadley wasn't won at a rescue mission in downtown Chicago. That battle had been waged for years on his mother's knees. In some family archives, we found an old photograph of Granddad Hadley when he was a young man. He was all decked out in a derby and the fashionable clothes he could afford before he lost his job due to his drinking. On the back is an inscription, written by his mother on "January 1, 1908":

> Oh, Will, every night when I read my Bible, I look at your picture, this picture, and I ask God to keep you and somehow heal your heart with His love. You may see this after I'm gone from this world and you'll know that I never ceased to pray for you.
>
> Mother

"I never ceased to pray for you," his mother wrote. That's where the battle for Bill Hadley's soul was won. It is where the battle for *every* soul is won. The dying people around you will make it home only one way. You will *pray* them home.

7
THINKING
LOST

"THE PEOPLE LIVING IN DARKNESS
HAVE SEEN A GREAT LIGHT;
ON THOSE LIVING IN THE LAND OF
THE SHADOW OF DEATH
A LIGHT HAS DAWNED."

⟨MATTHEW 4:16⟩

Jason wasn't part of our family, but he always made himself right at home. Like so many young people we have worked with over the years, Jason basically attached himself to our family. He was, in fact, the first teenager I was privileged to introduce to Christ after we moved to the metropolitan New York area years ago. He came to Christ on the night he had planned to commit suicide.

Jason felt so much a part of our family that he felt free to drop by anytime and, if the front door was unlocked, come right in and sit down on the couch in the living room. Once I walked into the living room, spotted our guest, and said, "Oh, hi, Jason. Excuse me while I get my robe."

Our young friend eventually went away for a hitch in the Army, and shortly after his return, he came over to his favorite house on Baywood Terrace. Sure enough, the front door was unlocked and Jason walked right in and sat right down. A woman he didn't recognize walked into the living room, looked surprised, and asked, "Who are you?" To which he countered, "Well, who are *you?* And where's Ron and Karen?" Small problem: We had moved! Someone forgot to tell Jason.

Poor Jason. He made an honest mistake: He went to the place where we had always been, and we weren't there anymore.

Tragically, believers are making that same mistake when they attempt to rescue the spiritually dying people around them—going to where they *used* to be. But they have moved! In a world that is changing rapidly, the attitudes and focuses of lost people have changed dramatically. But our approaches often are geared to reaching the unreached where they *were* spiritually and culturally, not where they *are.*

Charles Colson's observation is insightful: "In a startlingly brief period, the West has been transformed from a Christian culture—in which the majority accepted basic Christian concepts—into a post-Christian culture."[1] Unfortunately, most of our approaches to reaching the lost were developed four to six decades ago—when most people were familiar with and friendly toward those "basic Christian concepts." But people without Christ have moved. We are going where they used to live, and they're not there anymore!

Most of us who are in God's lifeboat, already saved, are part of a huge Christian subculture, with our own radio and TV programs, music, heroes, seminars, and even vacation spots. But while we have been building the largest Christian subculture in the history of the church, we have lost the general culture. No matter where you live in the world, whether in a post-Christian culture like America and Europe (where the Gospel is something people "used to believe") or a pre-Christian culture (where the Gospel is virtually unknown), there is a great gap between the world of the church and the world of the lost. Most of us who live or work around unbelievers don't need a sociologist to tell us that—we can *feel* the gap. We can tell that lost people around us either don't know about Jesus, don't understand about Jesus, or don't care about Jesus. And yet their eternity depends on them knowing about and caring about Jesus.

BROADCASTING ON THE RIGHT CHANNEL

To be one of Jesus' twenty-first-century rescuers, we must know how to "think lost." That means we must understand how lost people think and feel so we can help them understand what Jesus did for them. The

Old Testament describes the men of Issachar, who were committed to establishing the rule of David, the rightful king, as those who "understood the times and knew what Israel should do" (1 Chronicles 12:32). Those of us who are committed to bringing the rule of the rightful King into people's lives also need to understand *our* times in order to know what to do.

Once we have allowed Jesus to help us see the people around us as He sees them and once we have prayed fervently for their rescue, we need to try to understand these people we are burdened to reach. If we don't, we could be like weather forecasters broadcasting a severe weather alert only on AM radio when the majority of people who are needing to take action are listening to FM. The forecaster may be sincere, the information life or death, but he isn't broadcasting on the channel they're tuned to!

If we are going to do whatever it takes to rescue the dying people we care about, we dare not miss them because we were broadcasting on our channel rather than theirs.

Thinking "lost" in order to reach the lost is not a radical new idea. It is at least two thousand years old. You can see it in Jesus' "Are you thirsty?" approach to the woman at the well (John 4), His use of culturally relevant word pictures in His parables, or His willingness to reach lost people at *their* party, on *their* street, on *their* lakeshore. Paul explains his effectiveness in reaching the unreached when he says, "To the Jews I became like a Jew . . . to those under the law I became like one under the law. . . . I have become all things to all men so that *by all possible means I might save some*" (1 Corinthians 9:20, 22, italics added). Christ's great ambassador clearly did everything he could to understand and relate to those he hoped to rescue.

Thinking "lost" is really thinking "missionary." Over the centuries, effective missionaries have made the effort to understand the culture, the language, the spiritual "location" of the people they were praying to reach. We can do no less when we have been called to represent Jesus in post-Christian culture that one missions expert has called "the most challenging missionary frontier of our time."[2]

God has chosen you to be a lifesaver for Him "for such a time as this." (See Esther 4:14.) It is a time unlike any other since, perhaps, the first century. But it was in that time that the message of Jesus exploded across the world and captured hearts everywhere it was presented. And while this is a time of great spiritual challenge for men and women who want to rescue the dying, it is also a time of unprecedented spiritual openness.

As we commit ourselves to turn our lifeboat around to do the lifesaving work of Jesus, it is critical that we take the lifeboat to where the dying people are. Whether they work at the desk next to ours, live in the house next to ours, or sit next to us in class, they live in a world that is spiritually very far from ours. A world we need to understand.

FIVE SENTENCES THAT DEFINE MODERN LOSTNESS

There is a "new unbeliever" who is a product of the multiple moral and spiritual revolutions that have shaken our world in the past four decades. The baby boomer generation (born between 1946 and 1964), for example, has been described in a *Time* magazine cover story as "The Generation that Forgot God."[3] The worldview of many of the people we hope to reach can be variously described as post-Christian, postmodern, secular humanist, hedonist, or spiritually eclectic. All those descriptions may be true, but the heart of "where they live" can be expressed in five sentences that define modern lostness. If we can understand what shapes the spiritual "location" of our lost friends or loved ones, we can bring the good news about Jesus right where they are.

Here are the five descriptions of today's lost man or woman. First . . .

THE LOST PERSON DOESN'T KNOW GOD'S BOOK.

A Gallup survey of America's religiosity determined that the number of Americans who said they had no religious training in their background grew from 9 percent to 25 percent in a recent twenty-year period, and that 49 percent of parents said their children were receiving no religious training.[4] In other words, about one-fourth of adult

Americans and about one-half of young Americans received no religious training.

Setting surveys aside, my conversations, and probably yours, confirm the biblical illiteracy of many otherwise well-informed people. There is little, if any, knowledge of basic Bible stories and facts. At professional football games in the United States, there is one erstwhile believer who attempts to insert some Christian influence by holding up a sign that says "John 3:16" in the stands. As the camera catches that sign, I know many people have no idea who John is, why there's a three, a sixteen, or a colon. As far as they know, some fan is looking for his friend in Row 3, Seat 16!

I once heard Christian apologist Norman Geisler recount his experience when he was on a tour of the Supreme Court Building in Washington, D. C. He saw the Ten Commandments on the wall behind the Chief Justice's chair. The guide, who was a young attorney, pointed out the "statements numbered 1–10 on the wall." Dr. Geisler asked, "What are those?" She replied, "I have no idea."

When my wife's mother was in the hospital fighting what turned out to be a fatal infection, my wife was by her bedside for many of those last hours. At one point when she did not want to let go of her mother's hand, she asked the nurse if she would look up the Twenty-third Psalm in Mom's Bible. It didn't take long to realize that this medical professional had no idea what a biblical chapter or verse were.

These are small "slices of life" that are indicative of a growing unfamiliarity with God's Book. And in pre-Christian settings as well, a Jesus-ambassador can assume little or no knowledge of what the Bible says. Does that mean that a believer explaining life's most important relationship cannot use the Bible? That is, of course, impossible since it is the Bible alone that reveals how to begin that relationship. Without God's Word, the good news about Jesus is just another religious guess.

What this biblical illiteracy means is that we have to tell why we are referring to the Bible rather than just citing it presumptuously. And that does not have to entail a long apologetic, giving ten reasons why the Bible is the Word of God. I have found that most people understand my use of the Bible when I simply explain that it is "the world's best-selling book—ever."

While it is so much more than that, this "cultural authority"—the fact that this book has helped so many people for so many years—is a quick, non-contentious way to introduce the Bible into a conversation. Having sensitively brought in the Bible, the intrinsic power of God's Word will take it from there. It, after all, is "sharper than any double-edged sword [and] penetrates even to dividing soul and spirit ...; it judges the thoughts and attitudes of the heart" (Hebrews 4:12).

Because more and more people we meet do not know God's Book, they sadly are defined by a second sentence describing a modern lost person:

HE DOESN'T KNOW GOD'S RULES.

In Western culture, the words *right* and *wrong* have been irrelevant for three to four decades. Generations raised believing there are no absolutes are beyond wondering what's right or wrong; they often don't know there is a right or wrong. Consequently, many lost people around us have little or no understanding of a word that is fundamental to our Gospel: *sin.* That is important for us to understand if we are going to effectively communicate God's lifesaving message to them.

This moral and intellectual climate of "anything goes" is not entirely new. Once again, some of the first Jesus-ambassadors faced it in the first century. It is a challenge that Paul met when he went to Athens. Some observers have wisely pointed out that the world you and I are trying to reach is much more "Athens"—where people didn't know the Scriptures—than it is "Jerusalem"—where people did know the Scriptures. In a sense, Western cultures have moved from being a "Jerusalem" for the Gospel to being an "Athens." And in Athens, Paul encountered thinkers who "spent their time doing nothing but talking about and listening to the latest ideas" (Acts 17:21) and who lived in a city "full of idols" (Acts 17:16). They had no objective standard by which to measure truth, so they essentially accepted *all* spiritual ideas as equal.

The only absolute in Athens seemed to be tolerance. Today we seem to live in our own modern Athens. Anyone who dares to say some ideas are "right" and some ideas are "wrong"—that some lifestyles are "right" or "wrong"—is violating the only absolute still in place, tolerance.

And when "Paul was preaching the good news about Jesus and the resurrection," these Athenian thinkers said, "You are bringing some strange ideas to our ears" (Acts 17:18, 20). Increasingly, the good news about Jesus sounds like "strange ideas" to more and more dying people. That does not need to stop us but only sensitize us to not assume these are familiar ideas.

Needless to say, this ignorance of God's rules poses a special challenge for those of us who carry a life-or-death message about Christ's death for our sin. Many people believe sin is a nonissue. So how do we communicate a message that answers a problem they are not aware they have, a problem that is defined in a Book they know little about?

We will tackle that question in greater depth in a later chapter. For now, suffice it to say that man's sin is not the most effective starting point for presenting the Jesus-news to today's lost person. Sin is an essential nonnegotiable of the Christian message; that cannot change, no matter how much culture changes. But what can change—what *ought* to change if we want people to care about what Jesus did on the cross—is the starting point for our message.

That starting point is the results of sin. For while sin is a nonissue to many lost people, its results are a major issue: incurable loneliness, disappointing relationships, an uncontrollable dark side, chronic emptiness, a lack of peace. The lost people around you may not care about the disease they have called sin, but they care deeply about the symptoms of that disease. They just don't know it's sin that causes the symptoms they are all too aware of. Ultimately, our unmet needs and unanswered questions are because of the "missingness" of God, and God is missing because we have run our lives instead of God running them.

Because of the growing divide between the world of the church and the world of the lost, there is not only an ignorance of God's Bible and God's boundaries, but a third characteristic of an unreached person today:

HE DOESN'T SPEAK OUR LANGUAGE.

Everywhere I go these days, I see these signs that say, *"No fumar."* The "no" part is easy enough for me to understand, but at first I wasn't sure if I was *fumar*ing or not. Of course, by now I have figured out that *no fumar* means "no smoking." With the rapidly growing Hispanic population in the United States, it is a smart idea to post the no smoking restrictions in the language spoken by Hispanic people, especially if you consider it important that they understand the information the sign is supposed to communicate. It is, perhaps, the fundamental rule of getting any message across: Communicate in words the "communicatees" will understand.

When the message is from Jesus and it is life-or-death information for someone He died to save, that person must understand the message. So we who bear His message must communicate in language our lost friend or loved one understands. And for most lost people in the world today, you can be sure they do not speak "Christianese," that religious vocabulary spoken so fluently by us church folks. When the average lost person hears the words we usually use to communicate life's most important relationship, he or she either has no idea what we're talking about or has the wrong idea of what we're talking about.

We describe this relationship as "salvation" or "being saved," without any thought of how that sounds to the unreached person we're talking to. In our spiritual world, Christianese words are used so frequently that we speak them without thinking. But in their pre-Christian or post-Christian spiritual world, Christianese words are seldom, if ever, used, and certainly not with any understanding of what they mean biblically. We'll say more about moving beyond Christianese in the next chapter; we'll learn how to communicate our rescue message in words dying people can understand. But for now, let's remember this truth: Part of "thinking lost" is realizing this language gap and retraining ourselves to explain our religious words in nonreligious words. It is unthinkable that an advertiser of any product would present their product in technical words only their "insiders" would understand. Commercials are carefully thought through to make sure the words communicate to the person the advertiser wants to interest in that product. With eternal lives at stake, we can do no less.

Just as we need to ask the Lord to help us see what He sees in the lost people around us, we need to pray, "Lord, help me hear what lost people are hearing when I speak about You." You are starting to think like an effective rescuer when you begin to hear yourself speaking the "Christianese" that you used to never notice.

Being understood is of great concern to an ambassador, and especially to an ambassador for Jesus Christ. Ambassador Paul asked of his friends, "Pray that I may proclaim [the mystery of Christ] clearly, as I should" (Colossians 4:4). Not just sincerely. Not just correctly. But *clearly*.

A fourth sentence describes a modern lost person:

HE IS A SPIRITUAL SEEKER.

Emory University anthropologist Charles Nuckolls poignantly captured the "searchingness" of today's spiritually uprooted person when he wrote, "People feel they want something they've lost, and they don't remember what it is they've lost. But it has left a gaping hole."[5] His observation appeared in a major cover story in *Newsweek* magazine entitled "In Search of the Sacred: America's Quest for Spiritual Meaning." Modern magazines, movies, and television talk shows often tap into this growing interest in spirituality. "One of two dominant trends in society today [along with a search for deeper, more meaningful relationships] is the search for spiritual moorings," pollster George Gallup reported. "Surveys document the movement of people who are searching for meaning in life with a new intensity, and want their religious faith to grow."[6]

Modern men and women seem to know that nothing material will fill that "gaping hole," so they have turned to the spiritual zone to answer nagging questions about meaning, personal worth, life beyond death, and personal renewal. Those are questions planted by God in the human soul, what Solomon called "eternity in the hearts of men" (Ecclesiastes 3:11), to draw people toward relationship with Him. Unfortunately, without the light of the Gospel, this search for the spiritual is often a groping in the dark on "a way that seems right to a man, but in the end it leads to death" (Proverbs 14:12). In fact, "the god of this age has blinded the minds of unbelievers, so that they cannot see the light of the gospel of the glory of Christ" (2 Corinthians 4:4). Getting the light to them is the job of believers like you and me, God's spiritual rescuers where they live.

Wade Clark Roof, reporting his research on spirituality among the baby boomer generation, observed:

> Caught at the epicenter of a cultural earthquake ... members of this generation are asking questions about the meaning of their lives. In their ongoing journey of "groping for a new language of spirituality," they talk excitedly of a buffet-style spirituality which includes offerings like creation spirituality, Eucharist spirituality, Native American spirituality, Eastern spirituality, 12-Step spiritualities, feminist spirituality, earth-based spirituality, Goddess spirituality, and men's spirituality, as well as what would be considered traditional Judeo-Christian spiritualities.[7]

Obviously, a buffet of such wildly contradictory ideas should give the consumer a miserable case of spiritual indigestion. But for a generation searching for spiritual experiences more than spiritual truth (remember, most believe there are no absolutes), the contradictions don't matter. And without any objective measure for truth, how can anyone judge a "spirituality" other than by how it feels? While some who taste these offerings may not suffer spiritual indigestion, they still are left with a deep, unsatisfied hunger.

The "gaping hole" is not filled by the twenty-first-century spiritual buffet. But modern seekers want to be able to continue to search. As products of a culture where there is believed to be no such thing as absolute truth, modern lost people are not nearly as interested in finding what's "true" as they once were.

That was vividly illustrated in a story I heard Ravi Zacharias tell friends of his ministry a few years ago at a dinner in northern New Jersey. Once Ravi addressed a wall-to-wall crowd of students at an Ivy League university, presenting in his powerfully persuasive manner the intellectual case for Christianity. For an hour afterward, according to Ravi, his associate engaged in vigorous conversation with four young men who were contesting argument after argument that Ravi had presented. The associate answered every protest skillfully and convincingly from the Christian perspective. Finally, one of the students—who seemed to be speaking for all of his fellow debaters—made this surprising admission: "To be honest with you, I think most of what that man had to say is true. And *I don't care.*"

"It may be true, but I don't care." That sums up the spiritual blindness of so many seekers around us. They want to run their own lives. They want to go with what feels good. They want to assemble their own "truth"—whether it is true or not. Does that mean those of us who have been positioned by God to communicate the truth of Jesus have been assigned "Mission Impossible"? Not at all. It does mean that many dying people within our reach may need something more than an evidential reason to consider Christ—they may need an experiential reason to consider Him. The apologetic many modern seekers will best respond to begins by *showing the real-life answers to real-life needs Jesus offers* more than by showing the intellectual evidences for Christian truth.

That is not to say that lost people don't need intellectual barriers removed before they will open up to life with Jesus. And traditional Christian apologetics is a valuable tool in opening that door. But many post-Christian seekers you and I know are not necessarily searching for what's true; they are searching for what works. And it is the life and the message—the "show and tell"—of a Jesus-person in their personal universe that has the greatest possibility of breaking through on that level. For many, the *peace* Jesus offers, the *unconditional love,* the *healing* of what's broken, the *power to change,* the *meaning*—those are the most compelling components in our lifesaving message. Of course, only what is *really true* will *really work.* And Jesus is so much more than the One who meets our felt needs. He is "the way and the truth and the life," and "no one comes to the Father except through" Him (John 14:6).

While the searching of lost people you know may be taking them on confusing and dangerous roads, it is good news that they are at least shopping in the right store, the one that says "Spirituality." But the bad news is that they are shopping in the wrong aisle—in fact, for many, in any aisle but the one that says "Jesus."

Many Americans watched Alyssa Milano grow up on the TV situation comedy *Who's the Boss?* Her adult roles have been far less innocent, including her role as a witch on the series *Charmed.* She speaks for many in her generation and even her parents' generation when she says, "The religions that held up fifty years ago don't really hold up for the younger kids today. They want something new to believe in."[8] That is not the verdict of a generation who has carefully checked out what

Jesus offers and rejected it, but of a generation who assumes that Christianity is what people used to believe.

Ironically, the modern seekers' disinterest in the Jesus-way has not led them ahead to a more advanced spirituality but back to a more primitive one. While the packages are new, the products inside are ultimately ideas spiritually educated people left behind long ago: pantheism, animism, polytheism. Our hearts should be deeply burdened as we watch the sad words of Scripture being fulfilled right before our eyes in the lives of people we know and care about: "Although they knew God, they neither glorified him as God nor gave thanks to him, but their thinking became futile and their foolish hearts were darkened. Although they claimed to be wise, they became fools" (Romans 1:21–22).

For all the spiritual openness of our seeking neighbors and friends, that seeking often leads to experiences with no lasting peace and ideas with no lasting answers. In all our Christian busyness, we must not miss the lostness of the seekers who surround us. And if we are bothered by the spiritual darkness many are pursuing and living in, we need to go the next step to realizing the major reason for that darkness.

One morning at one of America's premier summer conference centers, my family and I were walking through the hall of the main lodge. Others were also walking toward the dining room for breakfast when the electrical power went out. Suddenly, we were all plunged into total darkness. We moved slowly, groping our way down the hall, trying not to hold hands with anyone but our spouses.

Later we were told why all the power had gone out. It was actually part of a regional power outage that was traced to a power plant forty miles away. A squirrel had somehow managed to chew through a main cable and, boom, there went the lights. And the squirrel.

The real problem that morning of the long, dark walk wasn't the darkness. Those hallways are always dark by nature. No, the problem was the failure of the light. Similarly, the problem with the lost people around us isn't their darkness—darkness is always dark. The darkness is there largely because of the failure of the light, the failure of Jesus' personal ambassadors to expose more of the people around them to the light Jesus provides.

In the Athens of his day, Paul found people he called "very religious," though they were very lost, in a culture "full of idols" (Acts 17:16, 22). He introduced them to the God who made men and women so they "would seek Him ... and find Him ... [who] will judge the world with justice by the man he has appointed. He has given proof of this to all men by raising him from the dead" (Acts 17:27, 31). Out of Paul's courageous stand for Christ, Athenians—totally unreached people—trusted the Savior. In the Athens of this day, you and I know people who are very spiritual and very lost. They are pursuing many "gods" to find the "Unknown God" (see Acts 17:23) who is the end of their search, the One they were created by and created for. Their only human hope of finding Him is someone who will be their "Paul"—the ambassador who will go where they are and tell them about the living Savior they know so little about.

One final element of today's lost person should give us hope that the rescue is within reach:

HE IS READY FOR JESUS.

The lost people around us may know less about Jesus than the lost of past generations. But the great news is that they are more ready for Jesus than ever before! That's because the very factors that have made them lost have made them ready.

They don't know they're ready for Jesus, but the world they live in and the lives they live have prepared them for a Savior exactly like Jesus. In a world where so little is certain, they are ready for a Savior who "is the same yesterday and today and forever" (Hebrews 13:8). In a world where stress is king and peace is a dream, they are ready for a Savior who said, "Peace I leave with you; my peace I give you. I do not give to you as the world gives. Do not let your hearts be troubled" (John 14:27).

With so many breaking, broken, and hurting relationships, they are ready for a Savior who says, "He has sent me to bind up the brokenhearted" (Isaiah 61:1). With the inner weight of so many mistakes made over a lifetime, they are ready for a Savior whose message is that "everyone who believes in him receives forgiveness of sins through his name" (Acts 10:43). With less certainty about what happens after their last heartbeat, they are ready for a Savior who promises, "I am going ... to prepare a place for you. And . . . I will come back and take you to be with me" (John 14:2–3).

Spiritually dying people you know are ready for Jesus—if someone would only tell them what kind of Savior Jesus is. They know little about Him because they grew up in a world that has crowded Him off the screen. But the God who loves them with all His heart, who is not willing that anyone should perish, is not about to let them die without a chance to meet His Son. And, humanly speaking, you are that chance. You will have to take the risks of building a bridge across the wide gap between your Christian world and their post-Christian world. But it is the mission for which you have been prepared, positioned, and summoned by your Lord. You have nothing more important, more eternal to do.

IF ONLY THEY HAD KNOWN . . .

In his autobiography, playwright Arthur Miller described life with Marilyn Monroe, his wife of several years. Miller told of the time during the filming of "The Misfits" when "he watched Marilyn descend into the depths of depression and despair." As retold by author Donald McCullough, Miller

> feared for her life as he watched their growing estrangement, her paranoia, and her growing dependence on barbituates.
>
> One evening, after a doctor had been persuaded to give her yet another shot, Miller stood watching her as she slept. "I found myself straining to imagine miracles," he reflected. "What if she were to wake and I were able to say, 'God loves you, darling,' and she were able to believe it! How I wish I still had my religion and she hers."[9]

I cannot read that without feeling a deep sadness in my soul for what might have been. If only playwright Miller and movie star Monroe had known who Jesus really is and what Jesus really can do, how much Jesus really loves us. When hope runs out—and somewhere, sometime it always does—it is all so hollow, so lonely, so desperate without Jesus.

By God's grace and by your courage and obedience, someone you know is going to meet the Savior whose love can finally fill the gaping hole in his or her heart. And for them, the hollow . . . the lonely . . . the desperate will finally be over.

8
BEYOND
"CHRISTIANESE"

WE IMPLORE YOU ON CHRIST'S BEHALF:
BE RECONCILED TO GOD.
⁓2 CORINTHIANS 5:20⁓

For Greg, the "Church Zone" seemed more like the "Twilight Zone" at first. He was almost thirty years old when a woman he was interested in invited him to attend church with her. It was his first exposure to the world of the church.

That first Sunday happened to be a Sunday when the church leaders were serving Communion, which they referred to as "The Lord's Supper." Greg surveyed what was being served at The Lord's Supper and commented, "He sure doesn't eat much, does He?"

Greg is a pastor today, and he reassures me his pre-Christian comment was honest, not irreverent. In fact, he summarized his first experiences around believers this way: "I didn't understand *any* of those religious words they were using!" He was not an isolated case. In a Western culture that is more post-Christian than ever, there are fewer people than ever who understand the vocabulary Christians use so commonly, so unthinkingly. And when you consider that the message we believers are talking about is life-or-death information, we cannot muddle the message with words that spiritually dying people do not understand.

Imagine, for example, that you are in a large meeting in a hotel conference room. Suddenly, a man bursts in the door and starts screaming in Swahili, "The building is on fire! Evacuate immediately!" You do not move; neither does anyone else. You turn to the person next to you and say, "He's obviously sincere, and he seems to have something important to tell us. Of course, I have no idea what he's saying." The fire burns closer. The messenger with the lifesaving information continues to urgently yell out his message. But no one moves. As desperately as you and the other people in that room need what he is trying to communicate, you will not respond. You cannot, because he is not communicating in a language you can understand!

We know from God's Word that we who belong to Jesus are the messengers of His sin-rescue to people. But people we know may, as Jesus said, "die in [their] sins" (John 8:24), not because we didn't try to tell them about their Eternal Rescuer, but because we did not tell them in a language they could understand.

We speak our "Christianese" so fluently, so naturally . . . but the people who most need to understand it have no idea what many of our words mean. To unfamiliar ears, "born again" either sounds like a cult or raises the question, "What were you in your *previous* existence?" The word *Christian* is so devalued in our world that it is virtually meaningless to most people. Either they think they must be one by virtue of their association with some "Christian" religion or they have no interest in being one because of what they think *Christian* means. So an invitation to "become a Christian" is neither clear nor compelling.

Our "Christianese" encourages a person to "accept Christ as your personal Savior." We are so accustomed to the phrase that it seldom occurs to us that such a statement does not even register on the screen of most unreached people. The average person's concept of "accepting" a person is nowhere near the biblical imperative of putting one's total trust in Jesus. And the word "Savior" is seldom used in modern conversation, and certainly not in a way that clearly communicates what Christ did for us on the cross.

Asking someone to "receive Christ" is also likely to leave the unspoken response, "I have no idea what that means." Many years ago, people spoke of "receiving" a guest, but these days we "receive" a package or a letter. When we ask a post-Christian or pre-Christian person, "Would you like to receive Christ?" he or she will likely wonder what we mean. To add to the confusion, there are religious traditions where the congregants "receive Christ" every time they partake of the elements of Holy Communion.

Some of our most precious faith-words can be misconstrued, misrepresented, and misunderstood. A few years ago a popular bumper sticker read: "Jesus saves—but Moses invests." While such irreverence makes us wince, it does illustrate how confusing our words can be. For the people who may need Christ most, the call to be "saved" is largely baffling.

"SIN" AND "BELIEVE"— WITHOUT CHRISTIANESE

Sin is a word that has little or no meaning to people in a world where there seem to be no absolutes, no clear boundaries. When you play on a field that apparently has no boundaries, you don't see being "out of bounds" as being an issue. How can you be out of bounds when there are no bounds? We cannot communicate man's deadly condition or Christ's amazing rescue without a person understanding their sin problem. But using only that word, *sin,* unexplained in nonreligious words, will probably leave a lost heart unmoved and unaffected.

The Scriptures call a person to "believe in the Lord Jesus, and you will be saved" (Acts 16:31). Unfortunately, that word *believe,* which believers use so naturally, is too devalued today to clarify what a person needs to do to be rescued from sin's death penalty ("saved"). If you ask the man on the street if he "believes in Jesus," he will likely tell you yes. But the chances are he does not believe in Jesus in the sense the Bible talks about—total trust and commitment. Most people "believe in Jesus" the same way they believe in the law of gravity or the existence of George Washington or Napoleon. They will say, "What I've heard about Him is true." But there is no concept of a faith-transaction between them and Jesus any more than between them and Napoleon. So to simply explain the way to Christ as "believing" is to leave them with a map to heaven that is too blurry to read.

Repent. Salvation. Redeemed. So many of the great words of the Christian faith have so little meaning to the people who are spiritually dying without Jesus. Many of them are Bible words; but like any missionary translating the Scriptures into the language of a tribe they want to reach, we have to find everyday words that accurately communicate the Bible words.

The bottom line for a spiritual rescuer is clear: It is not enough to transmit the lifesaving message of Jesus. We have to *translate* His message!

TRANSLATING, NOT JUST TRANSMITTING

In 1956, something happened on a tiny beach in a jungle of Ecuador that touched and transformed the lives of tens of thousands of believers across the world. Five American missionaries had dared to go with the Gospel to a savage, primitive tribe known to the world as the Auca Indians (known to themselves as the Waorani). Their reputation was that no outsider had ever seen them and lived. The five missionaries— Jim Elliot, Pete Fleming, Ed McCully, Nate Saint, and Roger Youderian —felt a call from God to carefully, prayerfully bring to the Aucas the good news about Jesus.

After months of lowering gifts from their plane, and even receiving gifts back, they felt it was time to make contact. Pilot Nate Saint landed his small missionary aircraft on a tiny beach on the Curaray River. The missionaries called it "Palm Beach." After some friendly contacts with three Aucas who ventured to meet them, they hoped and prayed for the opportunity to meet more of the tribe.

Tragically, the next meeting at the beach brought a war party. In a matter of moments, the suspicious and fearful Aucas speared to death these courageous spiritual ambassadors, dumping their bodies in the Curaray.

Word of that martyrdom flashed across the world, appeared as a front-page story in newspapers across America, and even became the subject of a major *Life* magazine photo story. More importantly, the story was told and retold to Christian young people for years to come. The words of martyr Jim Elliot went right to the heart: "He is no fool who gives what he cannot keep to gain what he cannot lose." And many of us responded to the call to surrender our lives for the service of the Savior those missionaries had died for. Countless missionaries, pastors, and Christian leaders are scattered across the world as part of the legacy of their sacrifice.

But, in many ways, the most amazing part of the story came after the deaths of the missionaries. Jim Elliot's wife, Elisabeth, and Nate Saint's sister, Rachel, went to Auca country to finish what their loved ones had started. God had given them a love for the people who had murdered the men they loved . . . and, miraculously, the Aucas allowed them to live among them.

Their challenge was to begin to translate the Bible into the language of a people who had no written language. It took some thirty years, but the Waorani Bible became a reality. And amazingly, most of the missionaries' murderers are now *leaders* of the Auca church. Only Jesus has that kind of power!

A few years ago, I had one of the great privileges of my life, to stand on the beach where those five missionaries gave their lives for Christ and for the Auca people. I had gone there to produce a radio program that would tell this holy story to a new generation who had never heard it. Rachel Saint hosted my visit—she had lived among the Waorani tribe for some forty years. In the process of talking with her and with one of the killing party, I saw dramatically what can happen when a spiritual rescuer pays the price to translate the message.

One of Rachel Saint's great challenges was to communicate the idea of forgiveness. The Waorani had no word for *forgive;* actually, no concept for forgive. When a Waorani was wronged, he simply speared to death the one who had wronged him. Rachel Saint faced the daunting challenge of trying to explain the forgiveness of Jesus to people who had never forgiven or been forgiven.

But as I talked with Mincaye, who had been one of the killers but was now a church leader, I heard with my own ears how the message had gotten through. Speaking through an interpreter, Mincaye told me with a smile, "I am getting older now, and I am looking forward to seeing Jim and Nate and the others in heaven soon." He paused and then said earnestly, "What we did on that beach that day was a terrible thing. But Jesus has washed our hearts."

There it was:

"JESUS HAS WASHED OUR HEARTS."

A spiritual rescuer had come to people to whom the word "forgive" meant nothing. But Rachel Saint did what effective missionaries have always done. She found a way to say it in words the people could understand. So a man like Mincaye came to Jesus with all his sins so Jesus would "wash his heart."

Every missionary knows the life-or-death importance of the good news about Jesus not just being proclaimed but understood. We who have been divinely positioned by Christ to rescue people around us can do no less. We cannot fail in our rescue mission simply because a dying person we care about could not understand our Christianese!

Obviously, the need to translate is hard to miss in a foreign missionary setting where there is a clearly different linguistic language spoken. However, the need to translate the Jesus-story is easy to miss when our neighbors and friends speak the same linguistic language we do, but a different *cultural* language. The words of our Christian "tribe" simply have no meaning or the wrong meaning to the lost "tribe" right next to us. Many lost people assigned to us have no better understanding of *born again*, *saved*, or *accepting Christ* than Mincaye had of *forgive*.

The apostle Paul had two prayer requests related to the way he communicated Christ: "Pray that I may declare it *fearlessly*" and "Pray that I may proclaim it *clearly*" (Ephesians 6:20; Colossians 4:4, italics added). Those are prayers each of us should utter as we join Jesus in His eternal rescue mission.

SOME ARE IGNORANT ...
SOME ARE IMMUNE

This *translation imperative* is not just an issue in rescuing pre-Christian or post-Christian people; it is essential to communicating to religious lost people as well. While the unchurched may be *ignorant* of Christianese, churched people are *immune* to Christianese. That is a major reason why people sit in churches week after week, hear the Gospel presented, agree with it all, and never give their hearts to Christ. They are so used to the words about Jesus that they think they have Jesus. But Christ made it clear that many who say "Lord, Lord" to Him on Judgment Day, who claim to have prophesied and done miracles in His name, will hear these chilling words from Him: "I never knew you" (Matthew 7:21–23). Knowing about Jesus is clearly not enough to belong to Jesus; knowing the words is not the same as knowing the Lord.

Sadly, people who have heard countless calls to "receive Christ," "get saved," or "become a Christian" think that call is for someone else. After all, haven't they "been there, done that"? Not necessarily. They may be mistaking "been there, *know* that" for "been there, *done* that." They have Christ in their heads but not in their hearts. And "it is with your heart that you believe and are justified" (Romans 10:10).

Immunity can be deadly. There is great concern these days about how common antibiotics have become, because people can develop an immunity to a drug from being exposed to it frequently. When they need that drug to save their life, that immunity could cost them their life. It's true spiritually, too. People who have been exposed frequently to the lifesaving message of Jesus may become immune to the very message their life depends on—forever.

My consistent experience has been that Christianese "veterans" often realize their lostness when they finally hear the "old, old story" explained in new words. When the process of beginning a relationship with Christ is communicated in nonreligious words, many religious people will say, "Is *that* how it happens? I don't think there's ever been a time when I did *that*."

So whether you are representing Jesus in a spiritual "Bible Belt" or a spiritual "Blackout Belt," you have to move beyond Christianese to communicate the message people cannot afford to miss. One of the reasons three thousand people came to Christ on the Day of Pentecost was because "each one heard them speaking in his own language" (Acts 2:6). They heard the Gospel in words they could understand.

Jesus clarified our translation imperative in His familiar parable of the seed, the sower, the four kinds of soil, and the four kinds of results. The first three harvests were either snatched away, short-lived, or choked by weeds. The fourth harvest produced "a crop [yielding] a hundred, sixty or thirty times what was sown" (Matthew 13:8). As Jesus explained the kind of person each soil represented, He said in each case, it was "the man who hears the word." They all heard the word; the message was transmitted to all of them.

But the fourth human "ground"—the "good soil"—received the seed. This "is the man who hears the word and *understands it*," Jesus explained. "He produces a crop" (Matthew 13:23, italics added). Apparently, it is not just hearing the truth but understanding the truth that determines whether a person's life will truly be changed by Christ. And that means the words we use are decisive in our rescue mission from Jesus.

If we make the effort to translate the Good News into the language of the person who needs it, we can be part of a life-giving miracle. Just ask Rachel Saint.

A NONRELIGIOUS GLOSSARY
OF LIFESAVING WORDS

Jesus wonderfully modeled communicating in nonreligious language. Consider two radically different people with whom Jesus talked about spiritual matters. To the Samaritan woman who clearly had a sin problem (see John 4:17–18), Jesus began by talking to her about being "thirsty again" and "living water" (John 4:13). To Nicodemus, a man who must have thought his religiosity was enough, Jesus graphically portrayed the wholly new beginning Nicodemus needed as being "born again" (John 3:3). In our world, that phrase has become overused, misused, or misunderstood, but as Jesus introduced it to Nicodemus, it was nonreligious language!

At various times Jesus described a relationship with Him by talking about a grapevine, a wheat field, a little boy, a choice of roads, a shepherd and his sheep, and a wayward son. He brought eternal truth within reach by talking about it in everyday terms. And Christ has left us "an example, that you should follow in his steps" (1 Peter 2:21).

But most of us Christians are so used to communicating in our religious language that we need more than a *should* when it comes to communicating nonreligiously. We need some *hows*. With that in mind, here are some ideas of how to express some of the most important words of the Jesus-message in words a lost person can understand.

Sin. A good phrase for *sin* is: *"Running your own life."* The Bible says that "all things were created by him and for him" (Colossians 1:16). That includes you and me. But we haven't lived "for Him"; we have each lived "for me." Sin is so much more than what most people think it is —just breaking some religious rules. It is the spiritual hijacking of your life from the One who gave it to you. It is all those daily choices you make that are "my way" instead of "God's way."

Saved. Another, better way to express this truth is to say: *"Rescued by Jesus from the death penalty for running my own life."* The running of our own lives cuts us off from the very Person we were made by and made for. The sin-wall between us is, in essence, an eternal death penalty for us—our separation from God forever. But Jesus came to rescue us from the death penalty we deserve. "God did not send his Son into the world to condemn the world, but to *save* the world through him" (John 3:17, italics added).

Savior. The *Savior* can be explained as *"Someone who rescues you from a deadly situation that you cannot rescue yourself from."* Jesus jumped into our deadly situation, realizing there was no way we could rescue ourselves. Like a person trapped in a burning building or the rubble of an earthquake, we could not deliver ourselves. He came from heaven to save us from a spiritual death sentence. "This is how God showed his love among us: He sent his one and only Son into the world that we might live through him" (1 John 4:9).

Believe. Believe is: *"Holding onto Jesus in total trust, as if He is your only hope."* That is what every dying person does when a rescuer comes; he or she clings to the rescuer in total trust. Such complete trust is what makes Jesus someone's *personal* Rescuer from their *personal* sin. The person who "believes" in the biblical sense of total trust in the rescuer "has crossed over from death to life" (John 5:24).

Accept Christ/Receive Christ. For either phrase, we can say: *"Welcoming Jesus Christ into your life, realizing who He is and why He came."* The apostle John explained well this kind of welcome, this reception and receiving of Christ, writing, "He came to that which was his own, but his own did not receive him. Yet to all who received him, to those who believed in his name, he gave the right to become children of God" (John 1:11–12). The name *Jesus* means "Jehovah saves"; when we "believed in His name," we believed in the Savior who rescued us from the death penalty of our sins.

Born Again. Born again is: *"A spiritual birth experience that begins a Father-son/daughter relationship between you and God."* There is no way that we can have a relationship with a perfect God when there is a wall of sin between us. But because of what Jesus did on the cross, that wall can be removed. When we put our trust in Jesus to be our spiritual rescuer, the barrier separating us from God is removed and we are born into His family.

Repent. A good phrase for *repent* is: *"Turning your back on living 'my way' to living 'God's way.'"* That meaning of *repent* was clearly part of Peter's message to those who had witnessed his healing of the lame man at the Temple. "Repent, then," he said, "and turn to God, so that your sins may be wiped out, that times of refreshing may come from the Lord" (Acts 3:19).

A TWO-LEGGED BRIDGE

The one-hundred-year flood in our area wiped out a bridge a lot of people depended on. It seemed to take forever to get that bridge replaced, and too far to drive the very long way around to get to what was on the other side. In fact, many people didn't bother. It was just too hard to get to what was over there.

In a world that knows less about Jesus, His Book, and His boundaries than ever, there is a wide chasm between the people who are spiritually dying and the people who know the way to life. And many people are living and dying without Christ, not because they have rejected Him, but because they have never heard and understood what He did for them on the cross. With Christians speaking in words that only they understand, it is just too hard for a lost friend or neighbor to get to the other side—unless someone who loves Jesus and loves them decides to be a bridge between them.

Building a spiritual bridge involves "thinking lost" in the words you use to tell the Good News. When you "think lost," you try to hear what you're saying with the ears of the person you're hoping to rescue. If you do, you will begin to hear your Christianese dialect and how confusing it must sound. You know you are stepping up to be a rescuer when you recognize your use of religious words and your "Christianese alarm" going off in your brain. That's when you can start retraining yourself, however hard it is or long it takes, to say it "plain and simple."

When you begin to speak to dying people about Jesus in words they can understand, you are becoming a bridge they can cross to find Him. Yes, it is a long way from where your lost friend or neighbor is to where Jesus is. They won't make it without a bridge. That's why God put you in their life.

9
CONFIDENTLY COMMUNICATING CHRIST

I AM NOT ASHAMED OF THE GOSPEL,
BECAUSE IT IS THE POWER OF GOD
FOR THE SALVATION OF EVERYONE WHO BELIEVES.
⌐ROMANS 1:16⌐

It looked like a crowd of New York Giants and one New York *dwarf,* those times I spoke for the chapel service of our local National Football League team. It was obvious who the football players were—and which one was the speaker. I could look some of them in the eye only when they sat down.

But I am grateful for the many opportunities I have had to speak for NFL chapels over the years. The chapels are optional, usually held on Sunday morning before the team meal, and often surprisingly well attended. The players are very attentive and receptive, but it's also obvious that they are very focused on Game Day. Some come to chapel with their playbooks; all of them range in mood from tense to intense. After all, their careers, their bodies, their futures are on the line for just sixteen game days each season.

The Giants have always been kind enough to give their speakers two tickets to the game as a thank-you. Since those tickets are hard to get, that's a great thank-you. During my visits to the Meadowlands Stadium, the Giants' home field, my first impressions are always of the fans having all those tailgate parties in the parking lot. They're cooking their hot dogs on little grills, laughing loudly and acting macho, and downing their six-packs of beer. Many are wearing the numbered jerseys of their heroes, hoping, I suppose, that somehow they can be a hero vicariously. Each time I go I'm struck by the obvious contrast between the intensity of the players I was just with and the party-hearty attitude of the fans who have come to watch them.

That contrast becomes even sharper as those fans enter the stadium and the game begins. As soon as a player makes a mistake, Fanman is bellowing expert advice, boisterous criticism, and demands for the player to go somewhere else. Meanwhile, I'm thinking of the players, especially some who have become friends. It occurs to me that all the heroes in the stadium are on the field—none are in the stands.

It's so cheap to be a fan. It's so easy to criticize when you're in the stands. For the spectator, it's no risk, no pain, no sacrifice, no sweat—just a party. That makes me want to stand up and say something to Mr. Fanman with his big mouth and free advice. "Hey, buddy! Why don't you get out of the stands and get in the game!" If he took me up on the offer, I suspect he would be a permanent part of the Astroturf in about thirty seconds!

INTO THE GAME

I can't help but wonder if Jesus isn't looking up into the stands filled with His followers and thinking the same thing. Jesus has millions of "fans," Christians who go to His meetings, believe His beliefs, contribute to His work, sometimes cheering for His team, and sometimes criticizing the players on the field. But in the desperate battle Jesus is waging to save people from hell and take them to heaven, He doesn't need any more spectators. He needs players.

When it comes to the rescue mission of Jesus, most of those who bear His name are in the stands, watching others do the work of reaching the people He died for. That is why so many are going through their lives and right into eternity without once having heard and understood the price God's Son paid to save them. Every follower of Jesus has been given a position to play on His rescue team. Every believer has been divinely positioned to be His voice to some of the people He died for.

So, the challenge of Jesus to each of us who know Him is:

"GET OUT OF THE STANDS AND GET IN THE GAME!"

Deep in your heart, your hunger for greater significance, to make a greater difference, has prepared you for that summons from the Master. It need not be some guilt trip that "I'm *supposed to* witness." It can be a personal passion, planted in your heart from Jesus' heart, to join Him in His rescue mission and to help some people you love be in heaven with you.

The "game" is challenging. Many of us live in a culture where Christians have lost home-field advantage; we are now the visiting team. The culture has moved so far from the Word of God, the ways of God, and the church of God that people know little or nothing about Jesus; they cannot be reached *religiously*. But they can be reached the way people have been reached for twenty centuries: *relationally*. That is why the new front lines of reaching the lost are in living rooms, not giant stadiums; on campus, not on a platform; in personal conversations, not evangelists' sermons. Post-modern, post-Christian (or pre-Christian) people will have to be reached where they are. You already are where they are: in your neighborhood, at your school, at your workplace, in your personal universe.

It is to everyday believers like you that Jesus now turns and gives His promise and His challenge: "You will receive power ... and you will be my witnesses" (Acts 1:8). The Son of God is moving you from the low-impact position of being a spectator of what He's doing to the high-impact position of being first-string varsity! You are moving out of the passivity of the stands into the high-action heroism of the most important battle in the world!

YOUR CENTRAL MISSION:
DELIVER A MESSAGE FROM JESUS

To play your position effectively, it is important that you understand your central mission—to deliver a message from Jesus to someone He died for. And you never know when God will give you one of His natural opportunities to introduce someone to Him.

Chuck had such an opportunity recently. A tire salesman named Bob arrived at his office without an appointment. Chuck was very busy but at the front desk at the time, so he spoke to Bob, giving him some tire sizes and asking him to get back with a quote.

About two weeks later Bob called up for an appointment, and Chuck told him to come over. "Right after that my file server crashed," Chuck recalled, "so my energy was directed at fixing that problem and not talking to a salesman. Nevertheless, Bob arrived and we started to talk about tires, and also, unexpectedly, about Bob's personal life."

The timing wasn't perfect. Chuck hadn't really wanted to visit. But he was prepared with God's love, as Paul said to be—both "prepared in season and out of season" (2 Timothy 4:2). He explained what happened next: "I was able to tell him about the peace and hope that I had in my life because of Jesus Christ. Bob looked at me with tears in his eyes and said, 'I'm a miserable man. I have no joy and no hope in my life.'

"He explained that he was a very angry man. We talked about the Lord for a long time, and I explained who Jesus was and why He came. I bought some tires and Bob left.

"The next time Bob visited me, he had a wonderful story to tell me. He explained how when he left my office the last time, he went out to his car and prayed to ask Jesus to come into his life. He said he immediately felt all his anger leave him. It was so real that he told his wife about it, and later his coworkers saw the difference that Jesus had made in him."

Chuck also learned that the first time Bob had stopped at his office was not a planned visit. He was having a terrible day and had decided to just quit and go home. "But he said he was somehow drawn here; he sensed that there would be something for him." There was something, Bob concluded. "That something was Someone—Jesus."

Those are the kinds of divine appointments that light up the life of a believer who has stepped up to be a spiritual rescuer. They do not always have an immediate result, but they do leave a lost person closer to Jesus. Since our central mission is the delivery of a message from Jesus, we need to clearly understand what that message is and how to communicate it clearly, without the Christianese that is so natural for believers and so foreign to unbelievers.

This message of Jesus, the *Gospel,* is succinctly defined by God's ambassador, Paul. "By this gospel you are saved . . . that Christ died for our sins according to the Scriptures, that he was buried, that he was raised on the third day according to the Scriptures" (1 Corinthians 15:2–4). It is a message about our self-run lives, the death penalty for all that "sin," and what Jesus did on the cross to pay the penalty we deserve.

We do not need to wonder *what* our message is supposed to be; God has made that crystal clear. We do need to think through *how* we express that message, as Paul said, "clearly, as I should" (Colossians 4:4). In the pages ahead, we will walk through one way to present this Good News in words that any lost person can understand.

CONFIDENCE BUILDERS

Before we unfold the message, there are some important encouragements about the messenger—you. God reveals four easy-to-forget, important-to-remember factors in communicating Christ that are significant confidence builders.

First, the method is sharing. Your mission is not to preach the message; that approach focuses on the other person. "*You* are separated from God" . . . "*You* need Christ." Sharing is about "you and I." The focus is on the other person *with* you. "I discovered that what I was missing was God. According to the Bible, I was separated from God—you are . . . we all are." Same truth, different tone.

Sharing delivers Jesus' message "with gentleness and respect," as the Bible tells us to (1 Peter 3:15). The classic description of this sharing mind-set is more relevant than ever: "I'm a beggar; you're a beggar. I'm one beggar telling another beggar where I found bread." When you bring the Jesus-news with that kind of spirit, you are coming in humility, not arrogance. You also are making the person feel valued, not condemned.

Second, the persuader is the Holy Spirit. Thankfully, you don't have to persuade anyone to begin a relationship with Jesus. That's not your job. Jesus said, "When he [the Comforter, the Holy Spirit] comes, he will convict the world of guilt in regard to sin and righteousness and judgment" (John 16:8). What brings a person to Jesus is a work that only God can do. "No one can come to me unless the Father who sent me draws him" (John 6:44). He draws through the Holy Spirit. And that is a relief to us messengers. Our mission is to present the message of Christ; it is God's job to do the persuading. That removes a lot of "results pressure" that might otherwise paralyze us.

Third, the authority is God's Word. This is not a matter of your opinion versus the opinion of someone with whom you are sharing Christ. You are simply sharing "what the Bible says about how to begin life's most important relationship." You humbly but confidently present the Bible, and the Bible will take it from there. After all, " 'Is not my word like fire,' declares the Lord, 'and like a hammer that breaks a rock in pieces?' " (Jeremiah 23:29). And "my word that goes out from my mouth . . . will not return to me empty, but will accomplish what I desire and achieve the purpose for which I sent it" (Isaiah 55:11). When you sow the Word of God in a human heart, you are planting words that are "sharper than any double-edged sword . . . . [that] penetrates even to dividing soul and spirit . . . ; it judges the thoughts and attitudes of the heart" (Hebrews 4:12). You may not be able to see any immediate effects from presenting what God says, but, like a farmer who sows now and reaps later, you can count on God's Word germinating in the life where it was sown.

Fourth, the message is Jesus. The message you've been entrusted with isn't all about Christianity. It isn't all about Christians or all about church or religion or beliefs. The simple truth is . . .

THE MESSAGE IS
ALL ABOUT JESUS.

The first Jesus-ambassadors understood their message simply and clearly: He "told him the good news about Jesus" (Acts 8:35). You can go into a spiritual rescue with much more confidence when you know you don't have to argue comparative religions, Adam and Eve, or the mistakes Christians have made. You "know nothing . . . except Jesus Christ and him crucified" (1 Corinthians 2:2). You keep the conversation focused on one subject: It's all about Jesus.

The power of this Person-centered message came home to me in an unforgettable conversation I had with Tony several years ago. He was our children's junior high band director and one of the most popular teachers in the school. One summer I hired Tony to help us paint the interior of our house. We were taking a break in the kitchen when I said, "Can you tell me a little bit about your background?"

He really surprised me with his reply: "I grew up in a pretty tough neighborhood. We had three different ethnic gangs there and a lot of violence. In fact, five of my good friends died violently in one year. Two others are in the penitentiary." I asked the obvious question: "Then how did you turn out like you did?"

Tony hesitated for a moment, then lowered his voice as he told me, "Remember I said five of my friends died violently? One night a gang from across town came to our turf looking for a rumble, and we gave it to them. I didn't see it, but a guy from the other gang came at me from behind with a knife. He was just about to stab me in the back. My best friend since grade school saw it." Tony stopped, trying to keep his composure. Then he said very softly, with tears in his eyes, "My friend took my knife—and my life has never been the same."

It was deathly quiet in the kitchen for a moment. I told him I was sorry and that it meant a lot to have him tell me that. Then I said, "Tony, in a way, I have a friend like that. Because of all the wrong things I've done, I had a 'knife'—a death penalty—coming from God. But when Jesus died on the cross, He took my knife from God—and my life has never been the same."

It is unimaginable that Tony would be ashamed or reluctant to talk about his friend who had died in his place. It must break Jesus' heart when we are ashamed to talk about the Friend who died in *our* place. The good news about the Good News is that it's all about Jesus. Our message is not about Christian beliefs or the Christian religion, but about *Christ*. And if Jesus, the only One who loved us enough to die for us, is all you have to tell about, it makes delivering your lifesaving message much less overwhelming.

A MESSAGE ABOUT A RELATIONSHIP

When it comes to presenting the good news about Jesus, "God did not give us a spirit of timidity, but a spirit of power, of love and of self-discipline" (2 Timothy 1:7). Knowing that we are His "glove" in presenting Christ . . . knowing He goes ahead to prepare a heart and create an opportunity . . . knowing that He wants to give us even the words we need, we have reason to be confident as we tell someone about Jesus.

And part of being "prepared to give an answer" (1 Peter 3:15) and "prepared in season and out of season" (2 Timothy 4:2) is to think through a clear, nonreligious way to present the good news about Jesus. Over many years of trying to communicate what Christ did to people who knew little about Him, I have found a way to tell the Jesus-story that lost people seem to be able to grasp and respond to. It is offered to you as an example of how you can deliver your lifesaving message in a way almost anyone could understand.

Since we cannot assume the interest of an unreached person in Jesus, it is more effective to start one step back from the Gospel—with a need that person can identify with. There is probably no life-arena that matters more to people today than the area of relationships—close relationships, broken relationships, bad relationships, needed relationships. And when the Bible describes our God-entrusted message as "the message of reconciliation," it is talking about a relationship message. *Reconciliation* is a relationship word, describing a broken relationship between two people being restored.

And since God is where we came from and God is where we're going, there is no relationship that matters more than one's relationship with Him. Consistent then with how important relationship is both biblically and to the people we want to reach, we can present the Jesus-message as how to have life's most important relationship.

LIFE'S MOST IMPORTANT RELATIONSHIP

Here, then, is the vital message of having life's most important relationship—a relationship with God the Father, our Creator.

All of us yearn for a certain relationship during the lonely moments. It's all about a vital relationship we've been missing all our lives. We know there's a relationship we don't have that we are supposed to have. Some think it's a best friend, a parent, a boyfriend or girlfriend. Others think it's a husband or wife, a close family, or children of our own. But every relationship ultimately leaves us with this hole in our hearts where "someone is missing." In fact, someone *is* missing. Our *Creator* is missing.

What the Bible says about this "Someone" who is missing can be summed up in only a few sentences. There is a relationship you're created to have. It's a relationship you don't have. It's a relationship you can have. But it's a relationship you must choose.

As a rescuer, you are presenting four key understandings about life's most important relationship. The first is:

THERE'S A RELATIONSHIP YOU'RE CREATED TO HAVE.

"All things were *created by him and for him*" (Colossians 1:16, italics added). In those six italicized words, God answers the fundamental question of our lives: "Why am I here?" You were created *by* Jesus Christ and *for* Jesus Christ. You will have a hole in your heart until you belong to Jesus Christ. The one relationship you cannot do without is a personal relationship with the God who created you. God loves you very much, and He wants to be in a close love relationship with you.

The reason we often feel so lonely, so incomplete, so confused about life's meaning is because . . .

IT'S A RELATIONSHIP YOU DON'T HAVE—BECAUSE OF WHAT YOU'VE DONE.

We were created to live "for Him." Each human being lives instead "for me." Isaiah the prophet wrote, "We all, like sheep, have gone astray, each of us has turned to his own way" (Isaiah 53:6). To put it bluntly, we are running a life that God is supposed to run. And He calls this self-rule *sin*. That monster called sin is at the root of our selfishness, our loneliness, our dark feelings, our guilt. Day after day we make more "my way" choices with our temper, our tongue, our sexuality, our relationships, the way we treat people. Because God is 100 percent sinless, we can't have a relationship with Him until our sin somehow gets removed.

In God's words, "Your iniquities [wrongdoings] have *separated you from your God;* your sins have hidden his face from you" (Isaiah 59:2, italics added). We are trying to live without the love and the life that we were created for, that only God can give. If we die with that lonely gap between God and us, it will be there forever because "the wages of sin is death" (Romans 6:23). The awful price for our sin is separation from God now . . . and forever. The Bible calls it *hell,* a place without God, without love or peace, and without relief. There is nothing more important in life than removing the sin-barrier between you and the Person who gave you your life.

Most of us know there's something between us and God. That's why we try to do good things to get to Him. But as any human judge can tell you, good does not repay bad. No matter how religious, how spiritual, how moral we are, it does not repay or remove a lifetime of "my way" sin-choices. Worse yet, doing good can never satisfy a *death penalty,* which is the "wages" of our sin. The only way a death penalty can be paid is by someone dying.

So, the shocking news from God is that there is nothing you can do to cross the sin-gap between you and Him. "It is by grace [undeserved love] you have been saved [from sin and its penalty], through faith— and this is *not from yourselves,* it is the gift of God—*not by works,* so that no one can boast" (Ephesians 2:8–9, italics added).

Your only hope is if *God* does something to bridge the gap. He has. As a result . . .

IT'S A RELATIONSHIP YOU CAN HAVE BECAUSE OF WHAT JESUS DID.

God loves you so much that He sent His Son, Jesus Christ, to pay the penalty for the sin in your life. "Christ died for sins once for all, the righteous"—that's Jesus—"for the unrighteous"—that's you—"to bring you to God" (1 Peter 3:18). The amazing Good News is that even though you did the sinning, Jesus did the dying, paying your death penalty for your sin when He died on the cross. "God demonstrates his own love for us in this: While we were still sinners, Christ died for us" (Romans 5:8).

But, of course, a dead man cannot be the rescuer, the savior you need. Again, the Good News is that Jesus Christ rose from the dead three days after He died. So Jesus is alive! The Bible says, "You, with the help of wicked men, put him to death by nailing him to the cross. But God raised him from the dead" (Acts 2:23–24).

The missing relationship becomes yours when your sin is erased from God's book. Jesus' death on the cross can bring you together with the Creator and give you His power to conquer the dark side that has always conquered you. You are ready for God when you can put your name in the most famous verse in the Bible, John 3:16. It's a statement you can make personal:

"God loved _____ [your name] so much that he gave His one and only Son that [if] _____ believes in Him, [then] _____ shall not perish, but have eternal life."

So the most important decision you will ever make is what you do with Jesus. That's because . . .

IT'S A RELATIONSHIP YOU MUST CHOOSE.

There's no such thing as a one-way love relationship. God did His part when His Son died for you. Now it's your move. Your move begins, according to the Bible, when you "repent, then, and turn to God, so that your sins may be wiped out" (Acts 3:19). Turning *to* God means you are also turning *from* something. If you want to turn to the sunset in the western sky, that choice will automatically turn you from facing east. You can't face east and west at the same time! It's the same way with Jesus and sin. As you turn to Jesus, you "repent." That means you are willing to put a self-run life behind you, realizing that Jesus and the sin He died for should not both be in your life.

In God's words, "whoever believes in Him [Jesus]" will "have eternal life" (John 3:16). When the Bible says "to those who believed in his name, he gave the right to become children of God" (John 1:12), *believed* means much more than just agreeing in your head. Believing in Christ is like a drowning person grabbing the outstretched hand of a lifeguard and saying, "You're my only hope!" You are "saved" from your sin and its death penalty when you tell Jesus with all your heart, "Lord, I'm pinning all my faith and all my hopes for forgiveness and rescue on You."

When you put that kind of total trust in Jesus to be your personal rescuer from your personal sin, the sin-gap is gone forever. The hole in your heart is filled. You are home.

If you want to begin this relationship you were made for, you can tell Him that right now by talking with God through prayer. You can tell Him that with the kind of commitment expressed in words like these:

"Lord, I've been running my own life, but I resign as of today. I was made by You and I was made for You, but I've been living for me. I'm sorry for that self-rule You call sin. But I believe Your Son Jesus Christ paid my death penalty when He died on the cross. And right now I am turning from a life of 'my way' and I am putting all my trust in Jesus Christ to erase my sin from Your book, to give me a relationship with You, and to get me to heaven. Lord, from today on, I'm Yours."

A REVIEW

You can summarize and scripturally support the life-saving message of life's most important relationship like this:

There's a relationship you're created to have. You were "created by him and for him" (Colossians 1:16c).

It's a relationship you don't have because of what you've done.

- Instead of "for Him," it's been "for me"; you're running a life God is supposed to run (Isaiah 53:6).

- So there's a chasm between you and the One you were made for, a chasm that separates you from God now, and ultimately forever (Isaiah 59:2).
- Because the penalty for running your own life is a death penalty, you can't pay it with your goodness or your religion (Ephesians 2:8–9).

It's a relationship you can have because of what Jesus did.

- You did the sinning; Jesus did the dying for those sins (1 Peter 3:18).
- You are ready to begin this relationship when you can put your name in John 3:16, saying, "God so loved _____ . . . if _____ believes in Him . . ."

It's a relationship you must choose. The sin-gap is removed and the relationship begins when you turn from running your own life (Acts 3:19) and put your total trust in Jesus to be your rescuer from your sin and its penalty (John 1:12).

A TITANIC MISTAKE

Each person you know who is living without the relationship they were made for deserves at least one chance in their life to take a walk up the hill—Skull Hill, that is. That's what they called the hill Jesus died on: *Golgotha,* or "place of the skull." Your wonderful privilege, your holy assignment is to take each one by the hand and lead them up Skull Hill until they are standing at the foot of Jesus' cross. For once in their life, let them see, let them understand how very much Jesus loves them, how very much He paid to be with them forever. The message is in your hands to deliver.

The ultimate tragedy will be if you make the mistake made that awful night the *Titanic* went down and 1,500 people died. Radiomen and the ship's officers chose not to deliver five of the six iceberg warnings received from other vessels. One was posted in the chart room earlier in the day, but that was later forgotten. When the message is life-or-death information, it must be delivered. Jesus has entrusted such a message to you and me. As faithful messengers, let us deliver it.

10
THE STORY
ONLY YOU
CAN TELL

Oh, no! Not another commercial!" That is the despairing cry of the frustrated television viewer. These rude punctuations of our entertainment are, of course, the real reason the program exists. Your favorite sitcom, newscast, or talk show is just bait to have you there for all those products being advertised.

But just when we thought we could not take any more commercials, TV invented a new kind of moneymaker—infomercials! If two minutes of commercials is obnoxious, what do you call a thirty-minute commercial? On many channels, advertisers can actually purchase an entire half hour, just to sell their product. They must pay off, for companies keep buying and producing more infomercials.

Many infomercial advertisers focus on a time-honored method of convincing people that their product is must-own stuff: the testimonial of a satisfied customer. If they're trying to sell exercise equipment, they have some star who looks like we want to look tell how the Herculiz-er made him what he is today. If it's a success seminar they're peddling, Ed and Edna Everyday tell how they went from welfare to Waikiki in just thirty days. If they're promoting a weight-loss program, they want Wanda Waslarge to show her wide-angle "before" photos and her current "lots less of me" photos. Her testimony that Weight Warriors made her disappear—and that the lo-cal shakes are out of this world—is sure to get the toll-free order line ringing.

Potential customers may not respond to a straight presentation of the facts about a product, but there is something compelling about hearing "someone like me" tell the difference that product has made. If you want to attract people to what you are offering, offer *living* proof that it works.

That principle also applies if what you are offering is a life-changing relationship with Jesus Christ. If you belong to Jesus, you are His *living* proof of the difference He makes in a life.

But note that the weight-loss commercial would have little impact if all the viewers saw was a slim person standing there, smiling. The TV audience has no way of knowing what the individual used to be unless the dieter tells them. The audience will never guess that it was Weight Warriors' program that made the person slim. Unless the person tells them, unless he or she gives a personal testimony. It's a story only they can tell.

Similarly, each Christian has a specific testimony only he or she can tell. You have a story like that. It is your Jesus-story. We have explored how to explain the good news about Jesus, the Gospel that changes lives and changes eternities. But it is important, as well, that a spiritual rescuer knows how to tell his personal Jesus-story, how to answer the unspoken question of many an unbeliever: "What difference does this relationship with Jesus make?" It is your spiritual story that can answer that.

THE POWER OF A PERSONAL TESTIMONY

When Jesus visited Samaria (John 4), He touched the heart and life of one Samaritan. Her story of what Jesus did made the local villagers want to hear Jesus' story. "The woman went back to the town and said to the people, 'Come, see a man who told me everything I ever did. Could this be the Christ?' They came out of the town and made their way toward Him. . . . Many of the Samaritans from that town believed in him because of the woman's testimony" (vv. 28–30, 39). They heard from someone like them what meeting Jesus was like, and they wanted to meet Him, too. That is the power of the testimony of one changed life.

God's ambassador Paul understood that power. As he stood before King Agrippa with his life on the line, he resorted to his personal Jesus-story. He told what he was, and he told what he had become. "I . . . was convinced that I ought to do all that was possible to oppose the name of Jesus of Nazareth. . . . I put many of the saints in prison. . . . I even went to foreign cities to persecute them." He went on to tell about how he encountered the living Christ on the road to Damascus and that he had traveled across the region and "preached that they should repent and turn to God. . . . I have had God's help to this very day" (Acts 26:9–11, 20, 22).

Notice the pattern of Paul's Jesus-story:

• This is who I was B.C. (before Christ).
• This was the turning point.
• This is who I am A.D. (after Christ); that is, the difference Jesus has made.

It is a pattern for all of us as we think through our own Jesus-story. Your testimony is not the Gospel. The Gospel is the story of how our sin has cut us off from relationship with God and how Jesus died to make that relationship possible. Your testimony is a living illustration, though, of the power of that relationship to change a life, the living proof that Jesus is alive and that a relationship with Him really makes a difference.

THE B.C./A.D. MIRACLE

When the twenty-first century dawned with blazing celebrations around the globe, most people probably missed the ultimate focal point of the party. It was A.D. 2000. That's *anno domini,* the "year of our *Lord* 2000." In other words, the world was celebrating two thousand years since the birth of Jesus Christ. For billions of people, human history is divided into two clear-cut chapters: before Christ and after Christ.

And for millions of men and women who are followers of Jesus, their personal history is a two-chapter story: their life *before* they began a relationship with Jesus and their life *after* Christ came in. As you think through the spiritual story that is uniquely yours, it is important to begin with who you were before you belonged to Him.

It is the B.C./A.D. difference that is Christianity's most powerful "advertisement." The blind man Jesus healed on the Jewish Sabbath had just met Jesus, but he really knew how to tell his Jesus-story. Badgered by Jesus' enemies to discredit Him for healing on the Sabbath, the man boldly declared the bottom-line impact of his encounter with Jesus: "One thing I do know. I was blind but now I see!" (John 9:25).

Had this man just testified, "I can see," people would have said, "So what? So can I." The "I *was*" part is what made the "now I can" part so amazing. To demonstrate the life-changing power of the Son of God, you have to present the what-you-were to what-you-are story. A temper that once was out of control but now is being tamed; a destructive trait picked up from a parent, now losing its grip; a habit or addiction whose power has been broken; a hurtful family relationship that is being healed—these kinds of first-person experiences of a living Christ act as powerful spiritual magnets.

Recently, I was standing nearby when Bill introduced his wife and three of his children to another speaker in a most unusual way. He said, "These three children wouldn't be here if it weren't for you." Bill then explained how this man had been the speaker at a Promise Keepers rally where Bill surrendered his life to Jesus Christ.

That was the night that his wife Laurie got a new husband. He *looked* like the husband who went to the rally, but he didn't act like him. Bill went home, made a lot of things right, accepted the responsibility for the unhappiness of their marriage, and let Jesus begin to change the kind of husband he was. A divorce-bound marriage turned around—and those three children all came after that miracle, three children who would never have been born but for the difference the Savior makes in a marriage.

Today, Bill is a compelling ambassador for Jesus the Rescuer as he tells people about what kind of husband he was B.C. and what Christ is making him A.D. He even helped to organize an area-wide conference for married couples. That is the kind of living proof a skeptical world is looking for—not just beliefs, but walking miracles. Unexplainable changes—except for Jesus.

OUT WITH THE OLD . . . IN WITH THE NEW

Every true follower of Jesus Christ has experienced some of those unexplainable differences. Basic to belonging to Christ is the exciting fact that "if anyone is in Christ, he is a new creation; the old has gone, the new has come" (2 Corinthians 5:17). Part of our preparation to be a rescuer of dying people is to clearly identify what "the old" and "the new" are.

"The Story Only I Can Tell" worksheet (next page) is a simple tool you can use to put into words your personal Jesus-story. The B.C. section—"Me before I met Christ"—provides an opportunity for you to think through the person you were without a Savior. Before Christ you may have been "blind" in painfully obvious ways, such as addictions, violent anger, sexual sins, or a vicious mouth. For many, the "old" was more subtle but every bit as sinful and hard to change; perhaps there was hurtful selfishness, family neglect, deep bitterness, or consistent deceitfulness.

What Jesus changed in you may have to do not only with what you did but with what you lacked—love to cure your loneliness, a purpose to give your life meaning, peace to still the turbulence in your heart, worth to give you personal wholeness, healing to release you from the pain of the past. Your Jesus-story begins with your identifying what was missing before Christ . . . and what was, indeed, impossible to change before Christ.

When golf champion Payne Stewart died in a plane crash, the world began to learn more about a dramatic change that had taken place during the last months of his life. One hint of the new center in his life was the "WWJD?" ("What Would Jesus Do?") bracelet he was wearing when he clinched his second U. S. Open title in June of 1999. Explaining to the media the impact of his new commitment to Jesus Christ, Stewart said, "I'm so much more at peace with myself than I've ever been in my life." After his win, he told *Sports Illustrated* that he had embraced Christianity "with the fervor of a prison convert." Described as "rude" and "arrogant" earlier in his career, Stewart said the peace he was experiencing was "wonderful." And he added, "I don't understand how I lived so long without it."[1] Several times at the memorial service after his death, friends referred to that "peace" which Payne Stewart had found in Jesus Christ.

THE STORY ONLY I CAN TELL

B.C. (Before Christ): A description of my life before I began my relationship with Christ

The Turning Point: How and why I began my relationship with Christ

A.D. (After Christ entered my life): The differences Christ is making

" . . . tell the people the full message of this new life." Acts 5:20

That kind of observable, flesh-and-blood difference is some of Christianity's most persuasive evidence. For that reason, it is important for every believer to think through the before and after of their coming into relationship with Jesus Christ.

As you prepare to share your Jesus-story with people who desperately need your Jesus, you begin by identifying who you were before He came in; then you move to describing *the turning point* where you began your relationship with Christ. What made you realize that Jesus was the answer you needed? What exactly did you do when you began your Jesus-relationship?

Your description of your spiritual beginning is a nonthreatening way for you to explain to someone how he or she can begin with Jesus—that's why it is important for you to walk through your beginning step by step, not just summing it up in Christianese code words such as "I was born again" or "I received Christ as my Savior." Whether you are explaining the good news about Jesus (the Gospel) or the story of how Jesus has changed your life (your Jesus-story), remember to communicate in nonreligious language.

Working through "The Story Only I Can Tell," you describe yourself "B.C."; then you describe the turning point that brought you to Jesus; and, finally, you describe yourself "A.D."—how you are changing because Christ is in your life. Most lost people you know will probably not be impressed by the fact that you go to more meetings now, abstain from "worldly" practices, or have a new set of beliefs. Their hearts are hungry, not to become more religious but to have the lifelong hole in their heart filled, to have their failures forgiven, to have some lasting love and peace, to make a new beginning. Your life, your testimony, is supposed to make people want to know "the reason for the hope that you have" (1 Peter 3:15). The transforming miracles in your life, your personality, your attitude, and your home equal hope for a person without a Savior.

REAL GOLD IN DARK PLACES

Some of your greatest opportunities to share the difference Jesus makes may come in the most difficult moments of your life. Virtually every approach to life works when things are going well. The acid test of what is real gold and what is fool's gold in life is your response to tragedy. As my friend Dave said after his beloved father's Christ-filled funeral, "If people without Christ want to know what a difference Christ makes, *let them come to our funerals!*" He's right. In those moments of some of life's greatest sorrow, we have some of our greatest opportunities to explain how Jesus has changed eternity from the great unknown into an exciting certainty.

When disastrous floods hit central New Jersey in September 1999 in the wake of Hurricane Floyd, whole neighborhoods were virtually wiped out. The floods did not spare the campus of Zarephath Chapel and Seminary; the church, the school, and the library were all devastated, along with several homes. But as usually happens to all of us when we are the victims of a tragedy, the spotlight was suddenly on our flood-ravaged friends. The media, especially New York-area television reporters, were all over the campus, shooting footage and capturing quotes. During the school's prior sixty years of ministry there, the media had barely noticed their existence.

Suddenly, in this darkest moment of their lives, everyone wanted to know how they were feeling. The believers there did an amazing job of explaining the difference Jesus makes when you lose so much that matters to you. Because their joy contrasted so sharply to the anger and bitterness of the flood victims interviewed in an adjoining town, the world was listening to this powerful proof of the reality of Jesus Christ.

SO OFTEN, YOUR PAIN IS YOUR PLATFORM.

During those moments when the bottom seems to be dropping out—the layoff, the breakup, the medical crisis, the close call, the parenting struggles—one of your first prayers needs to be, "O Lord, give me the grace to use this painful moment to tell them what Jesus can do. I know they'll be watching and listening to me as never before. Help me make the most of this hard and holy opportunity!"

Whether it is a hurting time or one of the many opportunities that arise from countless everyday experiences, our orders from our Lord are to "always be prepared to give an answer" (1 Peter 3:15), always ready to explain the Jesus-difference. We can find pure gold in those painful places.

For too many Jesus-followers, their "testimony" is limited to telling about when their relationship with Christ began. My wife Karen and I have been married for many years. Hopefully, I have something more to tell you about our relationship than showing you the pictures of our wedding day! It is all right to tell about how it began, but the real story is *what has happened since it began,* especially if you are someone who is single, trying to decide whether or not this marriage thing is something for you. Similarly, there is nothing wrong with telling about how your relationship with Jesus began, but the big story is how that relationship has changed—and is changing—your life today.

A CUSTOMIZED CONNECTION WITH THE LOST

That is why preparing for God's rescue mission includes building a testimony tool kit. When Paul talked about becoming "all things to all men so that by all possible means I might save some" (1 Corinthians 9:22), he was suggesting a customized connection with lost people, based on their interests and background.

In chapter 6, we discussed how to prepare your testimony tool kit. Remember the key principle is to customize your approach to the person. Your story of what Jesus did on the cross remains the same. It is only your *approach,* your *package* that changes. If a person is a parent, you will highlight how your relationship with Jesus has helped you as a parent. If you are talking with someone who is overdosing on stress, you can focus on how Jesus affects your handling of life's pressure cooker. Similarly someone going through a depressing time needs to hear the difference Christ makes for you when it's very dark. Someone dealing with death may be open to what your Jesus-relationship does to give you peace about eternity. Adjust your testimony accordingly.

My doctor friend, Doug, told me about a high school classmate he saw recently at their class's fortieth reunion. This very successful surgeon had never shown any interest in Doug's God-relationship—until this reunion. Having reached an age where he was thinking about his own mortality, the surgeon said, "Doug, I need to talk with you about what you believe. I'm nervous about eternity." A moment like that allowed my friend to reach in his "testimony tool kit" and tell about a Jesus who has made him secure about eternity.

One of Jesus' first ambassadors to dying people was a layman named Philip. Led by an angel of God, Philip moved from a large meeting where he was presenting Jesus to a remote desert road, where he would reach one searching man. The man was an official in the Ethiopian royal court, and Philip found him reading in the book of Isaiah. Admittedly, that gave God's ambassador a door of opportunity that was open very wide (Acts 8:26–31). But Philip's approach still exemplified the rescue approach Jesus used so often, starting at the person's own starting point. The Bible tells us that "Philip began with that very passage of Scripture." But he didn't stop at the spiritual point of entry. That verse goes on to say that Philip then "told him the good news about Jesus" (verse 35).

The Bible's account of this conversation underscores a point that has life-or-death implications for a lost person you care about. While your Jesus-story is a powerful place to begin, your Jesus-story is not "the gospel [which] is the power of God for the salvation of everyone who believes" (Romans 1:16). *Your personal testimony wins you the right to go on* and explain life's most important relationship. Wherever you begin, the life-saving "message of reconciliation" (2 Corinthians 5:19) that has been entrusted to you is where you want to go, as the Holy Spirit opens the door. Your Jesus-story demonstrates what a relationship with Jesus can do. The Gospel explains how a person can have this relationship they were created for.

Perhaps reading this, you would say . . .

"BUT I DON'T HAVE A STORY!"

That is the honest heart-cry of many Christians who have known about Jesus since they were little children. It's a little difficult to have a "once I was blind, but now I can see" testimony when you can barely remember not being able to "see." If you have always been a "good boy" or a "good girl," how do you tell a B.C./A.D. story about the *difference* since Jesus came in?

I am convinced that some spiritual "lifers" sometimes secretly envy those who have a deeply sinful past and, therefore, a dramatic testimony. If Christ delivered you from drugs or suicide or immoral living, the life-changing power of Jesus is obvious. But who is going to believe a testimony that says, "I was four years old, and I was in the sandbox—and suddenly I saw the light. Right there, I gave up sex and drugs and rock and roll." If you did not wallow deeply in the swamps of sin, what kind of story do you have to tell about being a "new creation in Christ"?

I am one of those who was intercepted by Jesus at an early age, and I didn't have much opportunity to do a lot of "big sinning" before I met Him. But in no way does that mean I don't have a story to tell about the difference Christ can make. Just because I began with Jesus early does not mean I do not have major sin-monsters stalking my life—or that I do not have a story to tell of the power of Jesus to beat those monsters. My selfishness can do so much damage . . . my words can wound so deeply . . . my temper can hurt most those I love most . . . my passions can pull me toward the darkness . . . my dishonesty can cost me trust . . . my dark side can mire me in depressed feelings.

In other words, I need a Savior, someone who can rescue me from the things I could never get out of by myself. And I have experienced what the Savior can do. He continues to rescue me from my dark side, changing me from the inside out, beating monsters that would otherwise beat me. So I have a Jesus-story—as much as a reborn addict who still has the needle tracks in her arms! Any longtime Christian who does not still find God's grace "amazing" needs to take an honest look at his or her own sinfulness. When you do, you—like one who was rescued from the "dirty," more obvious sins—fall on your face at the cross, overwhelmed by the love and forgiveness of Jesus.

Believers who feel they do not have a Jesus-story to tell can have such a story if they consider the sin-monsters Jesus is saving them from. They need to consider what their life would be like if it weren't for Jesus. In fact, I often encourage spiritual veterans to fill a sheet of paper, finishing this statement: "If it weren't for Jesus . . ." It is revealing to analyze the Jesus-difference in your life by writing out how you would be different if there were no Jesus. How would your lonely times be different ... your depressing times ... your stressful times ... your frightening times?

When you begin to think through what would be missing without Jesus, you are defining your Jesus-story. Remember, you *have* Jesus, and He is making so very much of a difference. And if life-change stories are convincing people to try weight-loss programs and exercise equipment, isn't it time your Jesus-story becomes God's instrument to draw people to His Son?

YOUR STORY IS NOT ABOUT YOU

I once read a story told by Dr. Harry Ironside, a respected Bible teacher of a previous generation. An Englishman in the nineteenth century went to London on business for a month, according to Ironside. Living far out in the countryside, he could not travel back and forth, so he bade his wife good-bye and set out for this extended time away—with a promise to write, of course.

After his first Sunday in London, the man wrote to his wife that he had enjoyed the ministry that day of two of the city's premier preachers. He had attended a "Dr. Carmichael's church" in the morning and at night Metropolitan Tabernacle, where he had sat under the ministry of the renowned Charles Spurgeon. I have never forgotten the man's impressions of these two spiritual giants: "Dr. Carmichael is a great *preacher*. Charles Spurgeon has a great *Savior*."

And that is the central issue for anyone who is representing Jesus Christ—as you have been divinely assigned to do among the people you know. Your life-or-death mission is not about you being a great Christian. It's all about Jesus being a great Savior! The story you have to tell is ultimately not about you. *It's all about Jesus.*

When a Samaritan woman breathlessly told her Jesus-story to her village, her testimony became an invitation: "Come, see a man ..." (John 4:29). She told her story so they would follow her to the One who *was* her story. And they did. "Many of the Samaritans ... believed in him because of the woman's testimony" (John 4:39).

By God's grace, many people in your "village" may believe in Him because of yours.

11
"NO GREATER HONOR"

"OPEN YOUR EYES AND LOOK AT THE FIELDS!
THEY ARE RIPE FOR HARVEST."
⁓JOHN 4:35⁓

She was only six years old, but Megan's question wrapped itself around her daddy's heart and wouldn't let go.

Her father, Mike, is a pastor. While he was studying in his office one day, little Megan came wandering in. She didn't interrupt her father's concentration; she just started looking around his office. She stopped when she got to the big chart of prophetic events on the wall. It's one of those charts that maps out a sequence of end-times events prophesied in the Bible. At the end of the time line are two groups of people: those with Christ going up to eternal life and those without Christ going down to eternal punishment.

Mike barely noticed as his daughter stared at that chart. She probably did not understanding most of what she saw. But she understood one thing. Breaking the silence in her father's office, Megan blurted, "Daddy! Can't you *see* it?"

"Can't I see *what?*" Mike asked.

Pointing passionately to the end of the chart on the wall, Megan asked the question that pierced her daddy's heart: "Can't you see all those people going to *hell?*"

Mike later told me, "I haven't seen all those people going to hell for a long time."

Tragically, neither have most of us who call ourselves followers of Jesus. Seldom does it occur to us that the people who will be "thrown into the lake of fire" (Revelation 20:15) will look just like the people we work with . . . the people we go to school with . . . the people we live around. Looking at those we care about and seeing only what our eyes tell us, we forget that it is some of them whom He will punish "with everlasting destruction and shut out from the presence of the Lord and from the majesty of his power" (2 Thessalonians 1:8). In God's own words, that is the destiny of *every* person who does not "obey the gospel of our Lord Jesus," which clearly calls on each one to "believe in the Lord Jesus, and you will be saved" (Acts 16:31).

That's "saved" as in *rescued from dying.* God is "not wanting *anyone* to perish, but everyone to come to repentance"; He "wants *all men* to be saved." So He sent His Son, "the man Christ Jesus, who gave himself as a ransom for all men" (2 Peter 3:9; 1 Timothy 2:4, 6, italics added). That's "ransom," as in the price it takes to buy someone back. The price to get us back was the eternal death penalty for all the sinning we have ever done. Hanging on the cross, cut off from God and experiencing every person's hell, the Son of God paid the awful price.

Clearly, Jesus sees "all those people going to hell" and He wants us to see them. He desires that we join Him in His desperate, whatever-it-takes life mission "to seek and to save what was lost" (Luke 19:10). When the late Christian musician Keith Green poured out his heart in a song called "Asleep in the Light," I believe he was pouring out the impassioned heart of Jesus . . .

Do you see, do you see, all the people sinking down?
Don't you care, don't you care, are you gonna let them drown?
How can you be so numb, not to care if they come?
You close your eyes and pretend the job's done.
Don't close your eyes and pretend the job's done.[1]

Because Jesus is at work in your heart—giving you *His* heart—I believe you do see people you care about "sinking down." You are ready, however inadequate you may feel, to discover your destiny in Jesus Christ by living to "rescue those being led away to death" (Proverbs 24:11). You are realizing who you are: Jesus' personal ambassador, appointed by the highest authority in the universe to represent Him in the place He has assigned you. You are ready to put the name of a lost person you know in that verse: "The Lord is not wanting _____ to perish"; and you don't want them to perish either.

God is preparing you to play your divine position in His plans to rescue some perishing people around you. It is the most significant legacy you can leave from your life. In the words of D. L. Moody, the man who probably introduced more people to Christ than anyone in the nineteenth century: "There is no greater honor than to be the instrument in God's hands of leading one person out of the kingdom of Satan and into the glorious light of Heaven."

THE MASTER'S "MIDWIVES"

Four of us went into that little room—and five came out. The room was a Chilton Hospital delivery room in Pequannock, New Jersey, and the four who went in were Dr. Steinberg, his nurse, my wife Karen, and myself. The one who joined us was the third—and final—little Hutchcraft, our son Brad.

And in spite of all the new lives he has helped bring into the world, Dr. Steinberg had apparently never lost the wonder. As our precious boy was born, followed by that amazing life-support system called the placenta, our obstetrician looked straight at me and said, "This is the greatest miracle known to man."

He was right—mostly. The birth of a person into a human family is the *second* greatest miracle known to man. The birth of a sinner Jesus died for into the family of God is the greatest miracle of all. At the moment of "receiving" Christ and "believing in His name," we "become children of God—children born not of natural descent, nor of human decision or a husband's will, but born of God" (John 1:12–13).

And, amazingly, at the point of someone being born into God's family, God often allows ordinary people like us to be His "attending physicians." Or more accurately, the Master's "midwives." Only a relatively few believers are skilled, trained, gifted maternity "professionals." Those spiritual obstetricians are the Billy Grahams, the polished communicators, the clearly gifted "soul winners." But those specialists will never be able to deliver all the "babies" that need to enter God's family. One reason so many people never make it is because we tend to think that all the baby-birthing will be done by those "with the gift" or who are "the type."

All over the world there are those everyday heroes called *midwives.* Midwives have brought millions of babies into this world! They do not begin to have all the training and expertise of a Dr. Steinberg, for example, but where there is no professional close enough to help a mom in labor, they do just fine.

Why do some people unexpectedly end up "midwifing" the arrival of a new life? Because they are the ones who happen to *be there* when the miracle moment comes. You don't have to have a professional baby-deliverer for a baby to be born. And that is a good thing—because often there is no professional there when it's baby-birthing time. In fact, the news occasionally reports one of those squad car deliveries, where some surprised policeman is suddenly the "midwife" for a baby who just couldn't wait for the hospital!

God may very well want you to be His "midwife," to assist Him in the delivery of a new person into His family. You may want to run for someone "better qualified," but you may very well be God's choice to help in the arrival of this new life. And "the one who calls you is faithful and he will do it" (1 Thessalonians 5:24). The Lord may well be preparing you, not only to *show* Him to someone who is lost, not only to *tell* that person about Him, but also to *bring* that person into His family. Yes, to actually deliver the baby.

But waiting until that moment to think about what to do is not advisable. It is important to think through how to help someone actually begin his or her relationship with Jesus Christ. In order to be ready to be a "midwife" for the Master, it is helpful to understand the *process* by which that life-giving miracle comes about. Every Christless person you know or meet is in one of three stages of coming from death to life. Your assignment from God may depend on which stages a person is in.

AMAZING DOIN'S AT HARVEST FARM

Knowing that most of us understand concrete examples better than abstract truth, God graciously reveals in Scripture His invisible lifesaving processes through clear analogies, including the harvesting of crops.

It is this harvest picture that enables us to understand what our spiritual assignment is in a given lost person's life, and what God considers "success" in our carrying out our mission from heaven. The process is clear in Scripture:

WE MUST SOW.
WE MAY WATER.
WE MAY REAP.

In preparing His disciples to be the "reaper" who "harvests the crop for eternal life," Jesus broke down the process into two phases: "One sows, and another reaps" (See John 4:36–37). The apostle Paul added a third step in the process: "I planted the seed, Apollos *watered* it, but God made it grow. So neither he who plants nor he who waters is anything, but only God, who makes things grow" (1 Corinthians 3:6–7, italics added).

So every person without Christ whom you meet is in one of three stages. If he has never really heard the good news about Jesus, he needs that message planted. If the message has been *sown* by some previous contact with the Jesus-message, the person needs at least to have the message *watered*. And if the individual has had previous contacts with the Gospel and/or with other Jesus-ambassadors, he may be ready to be *reaped*.

As a spiritual rescuer, your mission is clear: to leave each person closer to Jesus than he was before. Following the example of spiritual agriculture, you may be God's instrument to *plant* the Good News in one person's heart, to *water* the Gospel-understanding of another person, or to *reap* in still another life—actually guiding that ready person through the process of beginning their relationship with Jesus Christ.

Only the Holy Spirit knows how spiritually near or far a person is. "The Spirit of him who raised Jesus from the dead is living in you" (Romans 8:11). As you prayerfully "check in with headquarters," He will lead you into what role He wants you to play, what words He wants you to say to help a lost person take the next step. You just make yourself available each day to be God's servant through whom someone can come to believe. "The Lord has assigned to each his task" (1 Corinthians 3:5). He has a significant part for you to play in His courtship of someone He loves.

For someone, you will be the planter. Andy, a Christian attorney, stunned me with a living example of that planting step. As a teenager, he had been in a Campus Life group I led, he told me. Then he added, "You were the very first person who ever told me about Jesus. But I wasn't ready for Him then. Later, in college, when a lot of things weren't working for me, I began to be interested in that Jesus." I was thrilled to learn that today Andy is a wonderful Christian husband, dad, and attorney. I wasn't there for the spiritual harvest in his life. But, humanly speaking, there might not have been a harvest if I hadn't sown the first seed.

When my wife, Karen, was in high school, she had several classmates whom she very much wanted to have in heaven with her. Roger was one of them. He was in the school band, as Karen was. He was a drummer who marched to a distinctly different beat. Years later, words like "wild" and "crazy" seem to come up when people talk about Roger in high school. One day Karen tried, as best she could, to get her drummer friend thinking about Jesus. Somewhere in the course of the conversation, her concern for his eternity spilled over as she said, "If you don't accept Jesus, you'll be going to hell after you die." Roger's response was quick and withering: "Yeah, well, if you're going to be in heaven, then I'd rather be in the other place anyway!"

Karen doesn't remember that conversation. Roger has never forgotten it. Years later, my wife returned to her hometown and visited a church one Sunday. A man came up to Karen after the service and introduced himself. It was Roger, and my wife almost needed oxygen. After some quick reminiscing about high school days, Roger said, "Karen, I've been praying for years that I would get to see you again some day. I've been waiting a long time to thank you. You were the first person who ever told me about Jesus."

That "wild" high school drummer had come to the Savior in later years, served in Christian leadership, and established a Christian home.

Today—in the amazing ways of God—Roger works in our ministry, helping us to spread the Good News across the country and around the world through radio. And it all began with the sincere but awkward attempt of a high school girl to tell someone in her world about Jesus—and with a negative, hostile response. But that seed, however unskillfully it may have been sown, was later watered by someone else, and ultimately reaped in the beautiful harvest of a Christ-transformed life.

If God has assigned you to plant Gospel seed in someone's heart for the first time, you are not "a failure" if he or she does not agree or respond. You have succeeded if you have played the position God put you in that life to play. God may put you into the second position: *You may be the one who waters.* God may prompt you to speak to someone about Jesus because He knows the person has Gospel seed in her heart that needs to be watered. You will give her more information about a Jesus-relationship and perhaps pique her interest with your personal Jesus-story or clear up some misconceptions she has about Jesus. Again, your mission is to be faithful in playing your part, not measuring success by how they respond.

While only the Holy Spirit really knows where a person is on their spiritual journey, there are some things you can do to get a sense of their condition. Just bringing up Jesus allows you to get a reading of a person's heart. There really is "something about that name, " as songwriters Gloria and Bill Gaither put it, and your talking about Him may open up a window through which you can see into her heart. Asking a person to "tell me a little bit about your spiritual background" after you have told about yours may help you know how the spiritual "crop" is coming along. I find it revealing to talk about "the spiritual hole we all have in our hearts that is meant to be filled by a love-relationship with our Creator." Often a person's response to that provides a spiritual locator.

Because God works in unique ways in different lives, the harvest process is not always a long process. There are people who have been so prepared by God for the light that they are planted, watered, and reaped all at the same time. While that is not the norm, we as God's harvest hand, need to be ready to move at whatever pace the Holy Spirit is moving in someone's heart.

Sometimes the process seems to take much time, and the results are not apparent. But remember . . .

WHEN THE PROCESS DOES SEEM OVERLY LONG, DON'T GIVE UP HOPE.

Crawford Loritts once told about a professional football player who had been praying for his dad to come to Christ for years. The father followed another major world religion and forbade any talk about Jesus. But the Christian athlete and his grandmother never gave up praying for Dad. After years of a seemingly hopeless spiritual situation, this player found his father's heart finally soft—on his deathbed. Only minutes before Dad went into eternity, he opened his heart to Jesus Christ. I loved Crawford's conclusion: "As long as there's life, there's hope." If you love someone who seems like a spiritual "Mission Impossible," let God's promise be your solid hope: "Let us not become weary in doing good, for at the proper time we will reap a harvest if we do not give up" (Galatians 6:9).

Sometimes focusing on the planting/watering/reaping process becomes an excuse for not boldly presenting a person's need for a personal relationship with Jesus Christ. We can "cop out" by telling ourselves, "Well, I guess all I have to do is sow a little seed. I mentioned God once in our conversation; I did my part."

That timidity suggests that we have forgotten that the message entrusted to us is life-or-death information. Praying for an open door, an open heart, and words from God, we must "make the most of every opportunity" (Colossians 4:5) to present Jesus. And rather than secretly hoping that we only have to present the message, expecting that someone else will "close the deal," we should be praying that God will allow us to be His instrument to bring in the harvest. After all, harvesting is the purpose of planting. Catching is the purpose of fishing. A rescuer who realizes his mission is life-or-death would never be content to just point the way to being saved—he is determined to bring the dying person out!

So, sometimes you will be God's planter, sometimes His waterer, but there probably also will be times when He wants you to be His reaper because the field you're in is "ripe for harvest" (John 4:35). There is, as Moody said, "no greater honor."

KEY QUESTIONS

You have presented life's most important relationship to someone: the gap between us and God because of what we've done . . . the bridge across that gap because of what Christ has done . . . and the response of totally trusting Jesus as your Rescuer that begins the relationship a person was made for. The person you have been talking with has responded with an open heart, and you sense that he or she may be ready to make a commitment to Jesus Christ. That person is, as Jesus said of one seeker He met, "not far from the kingdom of God" (Mark 12:34). Not far . . . but not in.

With the Holy Spirit's inner "green light," you are at that moment when the seeker is inwardly asking, *What's next?* and you are asking, *What do I do now?*

How do you move from presenting the message to actually guiding a person through the process of beginning their relationship with Jesus? Some transitional questions may help both you and the seeker toward the next step. First, "Do you *want* this relationship with Jesus Christ? Should the answer be "no" or "I'm not sure," you can ask the person what would keep him or her from beginning the relationship they were made for. The reply may show you something the seeker does not understand or is struggling with. That provides you the opportunity to go back and carefully review the Gospel. Remember, it is the Holy Spirit who "will convict" (John 16:8), not you. Your heavenly mission is to clearly present, not to persuade.

When the seeker is able to answer yes to wanting this Jesus-relationship, you can ask a second question: "When do you think would be the best time to *begin* your relationship with Jesus?" If the answer is some form of "Not now but later," remind the person of the importance of making the decision now, while the time and sense of God is present. If a person wants this relationship, why should he wait one more day to have it? You might ask, "Why risk one more day carrying the death penalty for running your own life? God says, 'Now is the time of God's favor, now is the day of salvation' (2 Corinthians 6:2). He warns us that 'today, if you hear his voice, do not harden your hearts' (Hebrews 4:7).

Jesus tells us to come when God is calling us because 'no one can come to me unless the Father . . . draws him'" (John 6:44). If a person is sensing the tug of God now, then now is the time to come.

One last question brings a Spirit-prepared person right to the brink of rebirth. It is a reminder of the need to decide.

"DO YOU WANT TO BEGIN YOUR RELATIONSHIP WITH JESUS RIGHT NOW?"

Should he or she be reluctant to make that move at that moment, be sure to review exactly how the seeker can begin that relationship anytime, anywhere. Encourage him not to go to sleep tonight without Christ in his life.

Hopefully, this one for whom Christ died will be ready to let Him in: "Yes, I do want to begin my relationship with Jesus now." Assuming that praying is not a common experience for a person, it is probably best to assume that he or she is asking, "Exactly what am I supposed to do?" So you can help the seeker by telling him or her, "If you want to begin with Jesus, why don't you tell Him that right now?" Since "praying" may seem very intimidating to someone who has seldom, if ever, done it, it may be best to suggest "talking to God like you've been talking to me."

"If Jesus were sitting here right now, what would you say to Him about the sinning you've done . . . about what He did on the cross for you . . . about having a personal relationship with Him?" That is a good question to help a seeker put into words his response to what Jesus has done to remove his sin. If he says it to you, it may make it easier for the person to say it to *Him*.

The death-to-life moment comes as a person then talks to God, expressing his or her total trust in Jesus to be their Rescuer from their sin. In our ministry's Gospel presentation booklet *Yours for Life*, we offer this prayer as a way to put into words the desire to begin your Jesus-relationship:

146

"Lord, I've been running my own life, but I resign as of today. I was made by You . . . I was made for You, but I've been living for me. I'm sorry for that self-rule You call sin. But I believe Your Son Jesus Christ paid my death penalty when He died on the cross. And right now I am turning from a life of "my way" and I am putting all my trust in Jesus Christ to erase my sin from Your book, to give me a relationship with You, and to get me to heaven. Lord, from today on, I'm Yours."[2]

The best response is a prayer that comes from the seeker's heart, rather than from your heart or from a book. If it seems the heart is ready but the words just won't come, a prayer like the one above may help a seeker cross the line into God's waiting arms. While it is positive for you to pray as well, remember that your praying for this person will not bring him into God's family. Only his prayer can do that.

We have God's assurance that "everyone who calls on the name of the Lord will be saved" (Acts 2:21); that "whoever hears my word and believes him who sent me . . . has crossed over from death to life" (John 5:24); that "whoever comes to me I will never drive away" (John 6:37). The sin-wall between this person and their God is gone, and the relationship they were created for has begun!

And you have been there, assisting in the most supernatural event in all creation: the birth of a forgiven sinner into the family of God . . . the greatest miracle known to man. It is the unparalleled joy and high privilege granted to one who has seen "all those people going to hell" and stepped up to do something about it. This precious person you have led to Jesus will now be with you in heaven forever.

DYING READY

When Jesus was describing how people come into relationship with Him, He told a harvest parable that clearly tells us exactly what is God's job and what is our job in the process. He said, "This is what the kingdom of God is like. A man scatters seed on the ground." The seed is the good news about Jesus, and presenting that message is *our* job—with a lot of supernatural enabling, of course.

Then, "night and day, whether he sleeps or gets up, the seed sprouts and grows, though he does not know how. All by itself the soil produces grain—first the stalk, then the head, then the full kernel in the head." Clearly, that seed taking root and getting stronger in a lost person's heart is all *God's* job. Finally, "as soon as the grain is ripe, he [the seed sower] puts the sickle to it, because the harvest has come" (Mark 4:26–29).

The process of actually bringing in what God has gotten ready is up to us. That's why Paul, who wrote so fervently about God's sovereignty in saving us, was passionate about urging people to choose Christ. He said, "We are therefore Christ's ambassadors, as though God were making his appeal through us. We *implore* you on Christ's behalf: *Be reconciled to God*" (2 Corinthians 5:20, italics added).

Rick, our son-in-law, told me once about the grapefruit tree in his grandfather's backyard. Rick said that the tree bears a lot of grapefruit each year. But most of it never makes it to the table. "There's no one there to harvest them when they're ready," Rick said. "So they die ready."

Jesus told us that He has a lot of lost people ready for Him. "The harvest is plentiful but the workers are few," He said (Matthew 9:37). They're ready for Jesus, but if you and I don't go to harvest them, they will die ready. That is why Jesus has summoned you to join Him in His life-or-death rescue mission. You are better positioned than any believer on earth to rescue the dying people around you. To bring them home. To help change their eternal address from hell to heaven.

12
A ROAD MAP
FOR RESCUERS

"HE IS . . . NOT WANTING ANYONE TO PERISH,
BUT EVERYONE TO COME TO REPENTANCE."

⌒2 PETER 3:9⌒

Many news stories simply flash into our lives and then are forgotten almost immediately. Then there are those images that are embedded in our brains for years to come, like the dramatic rescue of little Jessica McClure.

Jessica had been playing in her aunt's backyard in Midland, Texas, on October 14, 1987, when she suddenly fell down the shaft of an abandoned water well. The toddler, only eighteen months old, became stuck in a sitting position at a depth of twenty-two feet. Rescue workers and emergency personnel descended on the scene. So did broadcast crews from across the country. Soon the eyes of a nation were on her life-or-death predicament.

It quickly became obvious that there was no way to get to little Jessica through the narrow well shaft. She was too far down, she was wedged in position, and the approach was too narrow. The rescuers put their hope in another shaft that they drilled parallel to the well and a horizontal tunnel they dug to access the well. The ordeal lasted a grueling fifty-eight hours. Many Americans checked the news at every opportunity to see if anyone had been able to reach this toddler we were all praying for. Those in America and overseas with news network CNN watched the cable TV outlet broadcast ongoing live coverage from Midland. Finally, at 8 P.M. two days after Jessica had fallen into the hole, the breakthrough moment came. A courageous rescue worker emerged from the ground with Jessica in his arms. Hundreds of workers and onlookers cheered—not to mention thousands of us who were watching on television.

Needless to say, the rescuers were hailed as heroes. They had undertaken significant personal risks and overcame daunting obstacles to get to someone who might have died if they hadn't. The one in danger was beyond their reach and difficult to access, but the rescuers knew they had to find a way to get to her. Rescuers always do. They know a life is at stake.

The mission to which Jesus summons each of the people in whom He lives is no less urgent—and no less difficult. God's 911 emergency call is to "snatch others from the fire and save them" (Jude 23). Given Jesus' description of hell as a place where "the fire is not quenched" (Mark 9:48), there is no more urgent work for you as a believer than to keep people you care about from going there—to snatch them from the fire.

Like the rescue of little Jessica, many of the people we want to reach with Jesus' lifesaving message seem beyond our reach and difficult to access. Living in a post-Christian culture where our lost loved ones know so little about God's Book, God's rules, and God's Son, we rescuers find a great distance between us and the dying people we must get to. If you are surrounded by people who are the "religious lost," you face the hardness of hearts immunized to Jesus by hearing about Him so much.

But when we see, through the eyes of Jesus, the awful lostness of the people we care about, we know a life is at stake. Like those rescuers of a Texas toddler, *we have to find a way* to reach them—no matter what the distance, no matter what the risks.

A ROAD MAP FOR THE RESCUE: JOHN 4

Thankfully, Someone has blazed a trail for us. Jesus Himself has become for us an exciting model of how to reach across seemingly insurmountable obstacles to bring someone to God. Jesus Christ faced rescue challenges very similar to the ones we face with twenty-first-century lostness, and He found a way to get to a spiritually dying person who seemed beyond reach. Actually, He found six ways—six lifesaving actions to rescue a dying person.

Our road map of rescue Jesus' way is found in John 4. Jesus was in hostile territory for a Jew—Samaritan territory. And one hot day at high noon He met a woman at a well whom many would have called beyond reach. But as the day ends, she has opened her heart to the Jewish Messiah, along with many of the people from her village. That is nothing short of amazing when you consider the walls between her and Jesus: a religious gap, a gender gap, a racial gap ("Jews do not asociate with Samaritans" [John 4:9]), and a moral gap (she was a woman who had slept with many men; He the sinless Son of God).

Our Savior showed us in a dramatic way how to rescue people who seem too far from us to reach. Facing many of the same kinds of barriers we do, His Great Samaritan Rescue shows us six lifesaving actions that can help us "snatch someone from the fire." In this chapter, we will look at the first three actions on the road to rescue.

LIFESAVING ACTION NUMBER ONE: ENTER THEIR WORLD

"He had to go through Samaria" (verse 4). That introduction to this rescue classic raises a question that would have been obvious to any Jew of Jesus' time: Why? Why would a Jew *have to* go through Samaria? After all, wouldn't a Jew want to take this direct route? No. In fact, because of the racial and religious hostility between them, Jews found every possible way to not go through Samaria. But Jesus considered it imperative to go there. Why? Because *you have to go to Samaria if you want to reach Samaritans.*

When we follow our Master's rescue model, we won't expect lost people to come to our turf. We will take the risks of going to theirs. To be sure, Samaria could not have been a particularly comfortable place for a Jew like Jesus to be. But since when is comfort an issue to someone who's trying to rescue a dying person? No one was ever rescued by a comforter in a comfortable spot! The firefighter has to go *into* the burning building; the earthquake rescue worker has to go *into* the rubble of a collapsed building; the lifeguard has to go *into* the surf where the drowning person is. And we have to go *into* the world of the lost person we hope to have in heaven with us. "The Son of Man came to seek and to save what was lost" (Luke 19:10). You can't save them if you don't seek them!

Because modern lost people, for the most part, have to be reached where they are, then you, as an "everyday Christian," become the key person for people around you. You already are where those lost people are. You are a disciple of Jesus Christ, "cleverly disguised" as a student at your school, a worker at your workplace, a neighbor in your neighborhood. For the dying people in your world, *no other Christian on earth is better positioned to rescue them!*

By making you His personal link to those people, Jesus has trusted you, elevated you, summoned you to eternal significance in their lives!

That is why it is so critical that you reach out to build meaningful relationships with the lost people you have been assigned to, and not to settle for just living in a Christian cocoon. The earlier chapter on "Getting into the Lives that Need You So Much" provides practical steps you can take to "enter their world," including opening your home to them, praying with them as the opportunity arises, and doing special things that will make them feel special. God will open amazing doors as you build intentional bridges into the lives of people He has given you to reach.

ACTION NUMBER TWO:
GO AFTER *ONE*.

I had just challenged a roomful of teenagers to pick a "target teen," one of their friends they would pray for and work to take to heaven with them. Janet rose to the challenge. She came to me and said, "I think the Lord wants me to try to reach Susan."

Frankly, I thought Janet had made a mistake. Like the Texas rescuers trying to get to little Jessica, I thought Susan was beyond Janet's reach. Susan was a "star" in her school: a pageant finalist, top student, and sorority sweetheart. Janet was a quiet senior, not particularly well known or active in campus activities. But she said God had laid Susan on her heart. How do you argue with that?

Three weeks later, Janet showed up at our Campus Life Club with an outgoing, attractive redhead at her side. Of course, it was Susan. The same Susan who gave her life to Christ just three weeks later. The same Susan who went home that night to tell her cheerleader sister Debbie about her new relationship with Jesus—who prayed to open *her* heart to Jesus that night.

Each of them—Janet, who started it all, along with Susan and her sister—asked God to lay one lost friend on their hearts. And the process continued. By the end of that year, I counted at least thirty-eight students in Janet's class who had come to Christ through the chain she had started—one life at a time.

In a way, something like that happened in Samaria that amazing day Jesus changed the life of a woman at the well. Jesus did not go into the Samaritan village of Sychar and start preaching on the streets. His strategy was not to initially try to reach the whole village. He simply focused on one. And because of that one, much of the village did ultimately come to faith in Him.

In the same way, Jesus is not asking you to go reach your whole office or neighborhood or school. He may very well want you to do what He did—focus on one.

When Andrew did that in Jesus' time, it started a powerful chain reaction. The Bible tells us that after he met Jesus, "the first thing Andrew did was to find his brother Simon and tell him, 'We have found the Messiah' (that is, the Christ). Then he brought Simon to Jesus" (John 1:41–42). Later there would come a day when that "one" Andrew felt burdened to tell about Jesus would preach a sermon where *three thousand* people would meet Jesus!

Only God knows the long-term series of miracles that could result from you praying a simple prayer: "Lord, please put on my heart one person You want me to reach for You." Your "Simon," your "Susan," your "woman at the well" then becomes a person you pray for by name every day, asking God to open those natural opportunities for you to show them and tell them about Jesus. Responding to this implant from God's heart into yours, you promise Jesus: "I will do whatever it takes to help my friend _____ be in heaven with me." It's a doable goal. It's a practical place to begin your commitment to be a spiritual rescuer. It's a powerful way to start a miracle.

ACTION NUMBER THREE:
CREATE SPIRITUAL CURIOSITY

With so many gaps between them, it was no small challenge for Jesus to find a way to open a conversation with this Samaritan woman. But He began by using the only real connection they had, needing water.

After startling her by asking her for a drink, in spite of the Jew/Samaritan wall, Jesus made this tantalizing statement: "If you knew the gift of God and who it is that asks you for a drink, you would have asked him and he would have given you living water" (verse 10). He did not start talking about her sinful relationships or introducing Himself as the Savior. He just threw out some "bait" that would make a fish start nibbling. He said something that would create spiritual curiosity.

Our Master told us to make people spiritually curious about what we have when he said, "Let your light shine before men, that they may see your good deeds and praise your Father in heaven" (Matthew 5:16). Not long ago, a veteran Christian college administrator came to me with a heavy heart and said, "I've tried everything to try to talk to my neighbors about Jesus, but nothing has worked." The good news is that this Christian leader realized that he was God's lifeguard for the "stretch of beach" that is his neighborhood. When he said he had "tried everything," I asked, "Have you tried random acts of kindness?" He thought about that for twenty-four hours until he saw me the next day and said, "That's it! I need to start building some bridges to my neighbors with some random acts of kindness."

It is, after all, the "good deeds" our lost friends see that Jesus said would ultimately get them thinking about our "Father in heaven." There are two kinds of good deeds that God can use powerfully to create spiritual curiosity as Jesus did at the well in Samaria: loving lost people in their language and being different in ways that matter to them.

In the midst of talking about proclaiming Christ's message, Paul told us to "be wise . . . toward outsiders." Then he explained what "wise toward outsiders" meant in the context of delivering the Jesus-news to them: "Make the most of every opportunity" (Colossians 4:5). That certainly must include . . .

LOOKING FOR OPPORTUNITIES
TO SHOW SPIRITUALLY LOST
PEOPLE YOU LOVE THEM—
IN WAYS THEY CAN FEEL
AND UNDERSTAND.

So it is part of our lifesaving mission to prayerfully ask, "What are needs I can identify in the life of the one I want to reach? What specific things could I do that might make them feel loved and cared about?"

Sometimes it's little things. In junior high, our son Doug had invited Marty, a Jewish friend, to go with him on a church outing to an amusement park. It wasn't a particularly spiritual event; in fact, the only activity that was in any way spiritual was a prayer for protection offered on the bus. But apparently that was too much for Marty. He went home and told his dad about it, and a chill suddenly ensued in Marty's relationship with our son. When Doug expressed to us his sadness about this strained relationship, we suggested to him that he buy Marty something to remember the upcoming Jewish observance of Hanukkah.

Our son stopped by the local candy store and spent about three dollars on a chocolate dreidle, a special toy Jewish children associate with the Hanukkah season. Two days after Marty received that gift, his dad brought him over to our house to spend time with Doug. In fact, his dad actually came into the house to talk to me—to thank me for the dreidle. Inwardly, I'm thinking, "It's no big deal. It cost $3.00!" But it *was* a big deal, as Marty's father explained.

"When we were kids in Brooklyn, there were two times a year we Jewish kids got chased and beat up—Easter time and this time of year, the Christmas season. They called us 'Christ killers.' So you have no idea what it means to have you give us this gift in honor of our holiday."

A simple gift. But, thankfully, it shouted, "We love and respect you" more loudly than we could have ever expected. The people around you need to be loved in ways that are customized to their lives, their needs. It might be free baby-sitting, homemade cookies, transportation, yard work, hospital visits, prayer in a painful time, a listening ear, a celebration of their special day—God will show you ways to express His love if you just ask Him to. And set against a world where everyone seems too busy to consider anyone else, those expressions will ultimately create curiosity about what makes you tick. And you will have the wonderful opportunity to tell them, "I just want to treat you the way Jesus has treated me. Nobody has ever loved me like Jesus does."

Alexandra was eighty years old when she began to realize that she could love people to her Savior. She had just lost her husband, who had "looked out for me in every way for sixty years." Alexandra said she had been feeling very lost, very lonely, and verging on self-pity.

After she heard me talk about Christians being the "make a difference" people in their world, she pulled me aside and told me she felt God was giving her a mission for the rest of her life.

"I live in an apartment complex full of lonely senior citizens," she said. "And I know how to bake cookies, to listen, to smile, to encourage people. So I'm going to get out of my cave and try to show some of Jesus' love to people like me." That kind of caring was bound to draw attention to Alexandra, and ultimately to the One whose love she was expressing. I loved her final conclusion: "My mother lived to be eighty-eight. That means I have at least eight years to really make a difference!"

Loving the people in our personal universe like that is the kind of "salt" that will make them thirsty for what we have. For who we have.

Another way to follow Jesus' model of creating spiritual curiosity is to be different in ways that matter to the people we are burdened to reach. For instance . . .

THE BEST WAY TO REACH YOUR PARENTS IS TO LET CHRIST MAKE YOU A BETTER SON OR DAUGHTER.

If you want to reach your coworkers, ask the Lord to make you the most conscientious, most caring employee in that workplace. How do you reach your neighbors? By doing the things that make you the best neighbor they have ever had.

Again, ask God to show you what change or difference in you would be noticeable and meaningful to the people you want to reach. They probably will not be attracted by the fact that you go to more religious meetings and cannot do some of the things they consider fun. To them, those are differences but not meaningful differences.

But they will notice differences that affect them—like an encouraging, affirming person in a climate of trash talk, a "pitch in" person where everyone cares only about their own work, a real listener in a preoccupied, interrupting world, or an always-honest person where believability and integrity are hard to find.

Wendy had been a Jesus-follower for only two weeks when she discovered the power of showing Jesus through a meaningful difference. Since Wendy was the first believer in her family, her big sister Laura was not buying this "new Jesus stuff" from her sister. So Wendy asked me, "How can I convince Laura that this is for real?" I suggested that she ask the Lord, "What change could I ask You to make in me that my sister Laura would have to notice?" This new believer looked at me and blurted, "I've got it!" and went home.

A couple weeks later, when I asked Wendy how it was going with big sister Laura, she said, "Great! I gave God the chair." The look on my face betrayed my bewilderment. So my friend went on to explain, "We have this big easy chair in our living room; it's right in front of the TV and right by the picture window. And Laura and I always end up fighting over who's going to get the chair. So I just asked Jesus to help me be unselfish about the chair. I let Laura have it all the time now. And she's been asking, 'What's *happened* to you, girl?'"

Two years later—harvesting often takes a while—big sister Laura came to me and said, "Ron, Wendy and I have some good news for you. I just gave my heart to Jesus." Before I could fully express my excitement, Laura went on to say, "But we've got a question. Now who gets the chair?" Amazingly, on the day Laura came to Christ, she was remembering what had first attracted her attention to Him—a sister who suddenly became unselfish about a chair.

That's the kind of meaningful difference that creates spiritual curiosity in a person who otherwise might have no interest in your Savior. The practical love you show the spiritually dying people around you, the practical difference they can see in your life, those are the keys that open hearts without Jesus.

LOVE FINDS A WAY

During those agonizing hours when Jessica McClure was trapped in that well shaft, rescue was clearly not going to be easy. Rescue never is—of a toddler in a well or a friend under the death penalty of sin. But those rescuers in Texas knew, as we spiritual rescuers must, that failing to reach the dying person is not an option. They found a way to get to that little girl. Can our determination to reach the dying people we know be any less?

I have always admired those four men in Jesus' day who were determined to find a way to get their paralyzed friend to the Master. The Bible tells us that the doors to the house where Jesus was teaching were blocked by the crowd. The windows were also blocked. There seemed to be no way to get the one they cared about to the only One who could change his life. But, like those rescue workers in Texas, they said, "There has to be a way!" And there was. The roof. They somehow managed to lift their friend up on the roof of the house, rip open the tiles, and lower him down, right in front of Jesus. (See Luke 5:18–19.)

Those four heroes seemed to have one passion: "We will get our friend to Jesus, whatever it takes!" It is that kind of holy determination to have a friend in heaven with us that will make us enter their world, focus on their eternal future, and do what we must do to create spiritual curiosity, just as our Master did one day at a Samaritan well. It's life or death, so . . . whatever it takes.

13
LIFESAVING JESUS' WAY

FOR I RESOLVED TO KNOW NOTHING
WHILE I WAS WITH YOU
EXCEPT JESUS CHRIST AND HIM CRUCIFIED.
~1 CORINTHIANS 2:2~

Like an Olympic track star crossing the high hurdles, Jesus leaped over one obstacle after another to get to lost people, no matter how far away they seemed. As we follow Him, we begin to see how we, as His personal representatives to the unreached people around us, can get to their hearts, no matter how far away they seem.

As we noted in the last chapter, Jesus' amazing mission to Samaria, recorded in John 4, reveals six lifesaving steps that can help us change the eternal address of people we care about. We have already looked at three of those steps. We should: (1) enter their world; (2) go after one, allowing God to lay one lost person on our heart; and (3) create spiritual curiosity before we present the message.

In an increasingly post-Christian culture that is not particularly concerned about sin, Jesus' next step becomes critically important.

LIFESAVING ACTION NUMBER FOUR:
START WITH THEIR STARTING POINT

Historically, believers presenting Jesus have made man's sin problem their starting point. Several years ago renowned psychiatrist Karl Menninger recognized a developing problem in referring to sin in his field. In his best-seller with the intriguing title *Whatever Became of Sin?* Menninger asked:

> Is no one any longer guilty of anything? Guilty perhaps of a sin that could be repented and repaired or atoned for? Is it only that someone may be stupid or sick or criminal—or asleep? . . . Anxiety and depression we all acknowledge, and even vague guilt feelings; but has no one committed any sins? Where, indeed, did sin go? What became of it?[1]

What Jesus did on the cross was for our *sins*. But in our post-Christian, postmodern culture, sin is largely a nonissue to people. When I was growing up, most people in Western culture knew and acknowledged a basic moral consensus, founded on Judeo-Christian morality. While many people did wrong things, they *knew* they were wrong. Today, that sense of wrong, of sin, has been neutralized by a culture that stridently rejects the "intolerant" idea that there is absolute right or wrong.

If the people around us do not understand the spiritual peril they are in because of their sin—and, therefore, their need for the Rescuer—they will, as Jesus said, "die in [their] sins" (John 8:24). So how do we introduce the Savior from sin to loved ones to whom sin is a nonissue?

The answer is right before us in John's account of how Jesus approached the woman at the well. Having shopped for love in one immoral relationship after another, she clearly needed to face her sin. Notwithstanding, that is not where Jesus began His message. He got to the sin issue, but He didn't start there. And therein is a powerful model for His twenty-first-century personal ambassadors.

Jesus launched into His spiritual pursuit of the Samaritan woman by talking about a need she cared about, thirst. First physical thirst, then the emotional and spiritual thirst she knew all too well. "Will you give me a drink?" (John 4:7) was His opener, followed by the suggestion that He could give her *living* water.

Then the Master turns the corner to revealing the problem with every "well" this woman had ever gone to for satisfying love. "Everyone who drinks this water will be thirsty again" (John 4:13). Think of that phrase . . .

> "THIRSTY AGAIN." THAT'S HOW EVERY EARTH-RELATIONSHIP, EARTH-ACCOMPLISHMENT, AND EARTH-POSSESSION LEAVES US IN OUR SOUL.

For a woman whose soul-thirst had apparently driven her from man to man, those words must have begun to open her closed heart. In creative, nonreligious language, Jesus made this offer: "Whoever drinks the water I give him will never thirst. Indeed, the water I give him will become in him a spring of water welling up to eternal life" (John 4:13). Jesus was offering an inner spiritual "spring" that would put the answer inside her rather than in "wells" she would have to keep going back to.

Jesus was showing all of us how *to start with the person's starting point, a need he or she feels.* When a person develops cancer, then that disease is his or her problem. But few patients walk into a doctor's office and say, "Doctor, I have cancer. What can you do for me?" They're not interested in medical attention because of the disease they cannot see but because of the symptom they can see. The patient is there because of a lump or headaches or pain.

While many of the lost people we need to rescue do not care much about the disease of sin, they care deeply about the symptoms of sin in their lives. They probably don't know it's sin that is causing those symptoms, but they are experts on the damage sin does. So otherwise closed doors open when we follow this Christlike approach:

BEGIN WITH THE *SYMPTOM*, MOVE TO THE *DISEASE*, THEN PRESENT THE *CURE*.

Every life without Christ is experiencing the symptoms of sin in some way, because sin cuts us off from the One we were made by and made for (Colossians 1:16; Isaiah 59:2). It is the "missingness of God" that is the ultimate cause of the deepest needs people are feeling. Here are some of the felt needs—the *symptoms*—that infect a lost life and open the door for Jesus, God's cure for our cancer.

- *Loneliness.* In a world of relationships that are superficial, unsatisfying, broken, or breaking, there is a deep sense of loneliness. A CBS news special on our "epidemic of loneliness" observed that "the loneliest place in the world is the human heart."[2] What we do not realize is that our loneliness is ultimately a cosmic loneliness. We're lonely for our Creator.

- *Restlessness.* So many people are afflicted with "destination sickness"—that awful experience of getting to what you thought would be a fulfilling life destination, only to discover that you still have no peace. In a recent interview, the lead singer of one of America's most popular bands said, "When you come from a place with no money, like I did, you think that's gonna solve your problems. . . . I still have the same problems I had when I started. . . . But now I realize it's really about finding inner peace. I don't have it yet."[3] That chronic "thirsty again" experience, that lack of personal peace, is a need people are painfully aware of.

- *The Dark Side.* The fourth *Star Wars* movie, "The Phantom Menace," had great marketing, including all the product tie-ins. One fast-food chain offered a cup that said, "Conquer the dark side!" That is easier said than done. Though few people know or care much about the problem of sin, most are troubled by their inability to conquer their "dark side"—their temper, their selfishness, their depression, their mouth, their addiction. While modern lost people may not be aware of violating God's standards, they are painfully aware that they have not met their own standards for how they should live.

• *Uncertainty and Insecurity.* With so much "up for grabs" relationally, financially, politically, personally, there is in many people a gnawing sense of unease and insecurity. We know that Linus minus his security blanket isn't much—and that all of life's security blankets can be lost. We are hungry for one anchor that cannot be lost. We are created for such an anchor—in an unloseable love relationship with the God who made us.

• *Pointlessness.* A recent *USA Today* survey asked Americans, "If you could ask a Supreme Being any question, what would it be?" The answers were very revealing. The survey showed that 16 percent of the respondents would ask, "Why do bad things happen?" A surprisingly low 19 percent would ask, "What about life after death?" And leading the way, with almost twice as many respondents as the next most popular answer, 34 percent would ask, "What is the purpose of my life?"[4] People are simply wondering, "What is the meaning of all this?" The only One who can answer the "why am I here?" question is the One who put you here.

Those are examples of the kinds of starting points Jesus exemplified in His Great Samaritan Rescue. You begin with a symptom your lost friends care about to introduce them to the disease and the cure that they don't care about. The symptoms of their spiritual cancer ultimately can interest them in a cure.

There is, however, one danger in beginning with a person's felt need: You may skip the cancer and go right to the cure. "You're lonely—and Jesus loves you. You're searching—and Jesus is the answer." But Jesus did not die to rescue us from our loneliness or our depression or our emptiness. He died to rescue us from our sins. So we dare not fail to communicate that the real issue is not our "lump," but our terminal spiritual cancer called sin. Paul's definition of the Gospel message is that "Christ died for our *sins*" (1 Corinthians 15:3, italics added).

While Jesus started with the Samaritan woman's unquenchable "thirst," He moved from that symptom to her sin. That is why He identifies that "you have had five husbands, and the man you now have is not your husband" (John 4:18). He did not start with the issue of sin, but He did not avoid it, either. We do not have the prophetic knowledge of the sins that may be in a person's life, but we, like Jesus, do need to move from the symptom that a person knows about to the sin Jesus died to save them from.

The Gospel never changes. Our starting point for presenting it is always changing—because we want to begin where a lost person is to bring them to the Savior they never knew they needed.

ACTION NUMBER FIVE:
AVOID RELIGIOUS TRAPS

Jesus was getting close to the Samaritan woman's need for a Savior. And she wanted to change the subject to talking about religion. "Our fathers worshiped on this mountain," she said, "but you Jews claim that the place where we must worship is in Jerusalem" (John 4:20). This rescue conversation was at risk of being detoured into a religious debate. But Jesus refused to fall into the trap of arguing religion. He quickly refocused the conversation on a person's relationship with God. "A time is coming when you will worship the Father neither on this mountain nor in Jerusalem" (John 4:21).

The issue, according to Jesus, is not our religion; it's our relationship with God Himself. Many of us who represent Jesus today have fallen into the trap Jesus so skillfully avoided. Our rescue mission is not to prove that our religion is better than someone else's or to defend our religious beliefs or practices. It's not even to convert a person to our religion. Our mission is to present "Jesus Christ and Him crucified" (1 Corinthians 2:2). A discussion of religious differences is bound to obscure that central message and polarize a conversation that could have been redemptive.

When a spiritual rescuer knows that what a person does with *Jesus* is the only life-or-death issue, he or she will keep bringing the conversation back to Him.

ACTION NUMBER SIX:
EMPHASIZE THE RELATIONSHIP

When American cruise missiles were launched at Baghdad during the 1991 Gulf War, they performed with deadly accuracy. In fact, one reporter on the scene reported that he saw a missile come in over the heart of the city, turn sharply to the left, and go down the smokestack of a military command building. That missile had apparently been able to read that it was slightly off course, correct its direction, and go straight to its target. The reason those missiles so often succeeded in their mission was their powerful internal guidance system.

For spiritual rescuers to succeed in their life-or-death mission, they have to stay on target and quickly correct themselves if they veer off course. And the transmissions from the internal guidance system of the Holy Spirit will tell you, "Stick to Jesus. It's all about Jesus!" The Master said of the Spirit, "He will testify about me. [And] you also must testify" (John 15:26–27).

Talking about religion is a detour. Talking about a relationship with God is the main road. As Jesus modeled effective rescue in Samaria, He quickly steered the conversation away from religion and back to relationship. He refused to talk about how their different religions worshiped; He talked instead about "the kind of worshipers the Father seeks" (John 4:23). Brushing aside the importance of religious practices, He said, "God is spirit, and his worshipers must worship in spirit and in truth" (verse 24). Again, it's how you relate to *God* that matters.

Ultimately Jesus brought the conversation to that truth by announcing that He, as the Messiah, was the issue: "Then Jesus declared, 'I who speak to you am he'" (John 4:26).

Did the woman grasp that it was all about Jesus? Her testimony to her village says it all: "Come, see a man. . . . Could this be the Christ?" (John 4:29). She went to her neighbors, not with a message about a religion or beliefs, but about the man Jesus.

Our daughter, Lisa, had to be a spiritual "cruise missile" one day when the discussion in her English class turned to religion. The teacher asked, "How many of you believe in something so strongly that you would die for it?" One lonesome hand went up; it was Lisa's. The teacher followed up by asking, "Lisa, what would you be willing to die for?"

"For my relationship with Jesus Christ," she answered bravely.

Not ready to let the exchange end there, the teacher said, "Class, how many of you would be willing to die for your religion?" Lisa raised her hand again and asked to speak.

"Actually," she began, "I wouldn't die for my religion. I said I would die for my relationship with Jesus Christ."

For most people, any belief about God or Christ is because that is what your religion says. Jesus and "religion" are synonyms in most people's minds. But . . .

JESUS IS A PERSON SEEKING A LOVE RELATIONSHIP WITH US, NOT A SYSTEM SEEKING ADHERENTS OR DICTATING REQUIREMENTS.

The only way spiritually dying people are going to understand the difference is if we as Christ's ambassadors continue to stay on the message, *to emphasizes this is a relationship.*

There is nothing strange about someone talking about the valued relationships in their life. Grandparents naturally talk about their grandchildren; boyfriends and girlfriends naturally talk about each other; husbands and wives will, of course, talk about the love of their life. That is what is so exciting, so liberating about the message with which you have been entrusted by the Savior. It is not about changing someone's religion, getting someone to sign up for your beliefs, or winning a spiritual debate. It is simply you telling someone who's important to you about the most important relationship in your life . . . your relationship with the only One who ever loved you enough to die for you.

Your rescue mission is not really complicated. You are taking Jesus by one hand and someone you care about by the other hand—and bringing them together. Forever.

WAITING AT THE GATE

I was at O'Hare International Airport in Chicago, waiting for my flight in the lounge of Gate B6. But before the passengers for my flight could board, the incoming passengers had to disembark. I hadn't ex-

166

pected to see the unforgettable, emotional scene that unfolded as I watched.

It was shortly after the Gulf War had ended, and soldiers were coming home. Clustered anxiously around the end of the Jetway were a boy in a Desert Storm T-shirt, a little girl, a wife carrying a flag with a yellow ribbon attached, and a friend with a video camera aimed down the Jetway. The wife was crying what must have been tears of anxious anticipation as her son hung on the corner of the Jetway door, peeking down the tunnel. It was hard not to watch, and many people in the lounge were doing just that—some even wiping their eyes.

As more and more passengers streamed off the plane, the wife was fighting more and more to keep her composure. Then, as a flight attendant came out, the wife asked painfully, "Are there any more passengers?" "Only a few" was her disappointing answer. Moments later, as the last passenger left, that precious wife fell into a chair and melted into tears. It had been a heartbreaking moment. The anticipated reunion didn't happen; the one she wanted home didn't come.

I can't help but wonder if there will be scenes like that in heaven, as we look anxiously to see if someone we love made it home. Jesus did all He could do to bring them home to heaven. Now it's in our hands to do all we can.

14
REMOVING
THE ROADBLOCKS

"WILL HE NOT LEAVE THE NINETY-NINE ON THE HILLS
AND GO TO LOOK FOR THE ONE THAT WANDERED OFF?"
⌐MATTHEW 18:12⌐

Alfred Rascon was a twenty-one-year-old medic on March 16, 1966, the day his platoon came under heavy attack in a Vietnamese jungle. He saw a fellow soldier cut down by enemy bullets and moved quickly to try to rescue him. Suddenly, Rascon felt a bullet slice into his hip. Then a grenade exploded in his face, leaving several shrapnel wounds.

But he couldn't stop. Despite his wounds, the courageous medic dragged his fallen colleague to safety. The battle continued to rage, and Alfred Rascon continued to fight for his comrades. He delivered ammunition to a machine gunner, then covered two badly wounded soldiers with his body, absorbing grenade blasts and saving both their lives.[1]

His government later acknowledged his heroism with the U. S. Medal of Honor, presented by the president of the United States. And Alfred Rascon was a genuine hero. Even though bullets were flying all around him, even though he was wounded himself, even though it might cost him his life—he let nothing stop him in his battle to save the lives of others.

But then, that is often the story of rescue heroes. When a federal building in Oklahoma City was blown up by terrorists, the rescue workers risked themselves to go into a seriously damaged building that could collapse upon them in order to find the people who were trapped underneath. When an earthquake devastates a building, rescuers dig through whatever stands between them and the dying people inside, never knowing if and when an aftershock could bring the rest of the structure down on them.

When you know people may die if you don't get to them, no risk, no obstacle, no injury can make you give up. There's a life at stake. It is that kind of self-forgetting heroism that turns everyday people into uncommon heroes.

In the battle for a spiritually dying person, desperately in need of Jesus, we realize someone may die forever if we don't bring the person out. Not that there aren't obstacles to overcome. There are barriers to remove and rubble to dig through before we can reach a dying loved one. And just like that courageous medic who saved three lives in combat, we cannot let the bullets or the wounds stop us. There's a life at stake.

EXPECT ROADBLOCKS
DURING THE RESCUE EFFORT

As you point someone in your "rescue zone" toward Jesus, expect some obstacles. They may come in the form of objections or questions or misconceptions that arise when people hear the good news about Jesus. And there's a reason, according to the apostle Paul. "The god of this age has blinded the minds of unbelievers, so that they cannot see the light of the gospel of the glory of Christ" (2 Corinthians 4:4). When a lost heart suddenly starts to consider Jesus, Satan goes on high alert to fight to keep his prisoner. He is, as Jesus told us, "the father of lies" (John 8:44), and he uses some of his lies to blind unbelievers to the light of Christ.

As you try to present life's most important relationship to someone, you are often challenged by your lost friend with some question or objection, usually one that has been raised by countless seekers over the centuries. It is often at that point, when the bullets start flying, that we are tempted to retreat. But that's not an option when a life is at stake. And since there are certain obstacles that continually come up in conversations about Jesus, it is possible to prepare yourself to overcome those obstacles. They are, in essence, roadblocks on the road to heaven for someone you care about.

Since the battle for a human heart is ultimately "not against flesh and blood" but "against the devil's schemes" (Ephesians 6:11–12), a spiritual rescuer must remember that "the weapons we fight with are not the weapons of the world" (2 Corinthians 10:4). Removing rescue roadblocks is not a matter of human cleverness or persuasion. It is not about winning a spiritual argument or prevailing with an irrefutable answer. Those "earth-weapons" cannot prevail against the devil's deceits and distractions. "On the contrary, [the weapons we fight with] have divine power to demolish strongholds. We demolish arguments and every pretension that sets itself up against the knowledge of God" (verses 4–5).

This divine power is ours through prayer. Indeed . . .

EVERY BATTLE FOR SOMEONE'S ETERNITY IS ULTIMATELY WON ON OUR KNEES.

By "wrestling in prayer" (Colossians 4:12) for someone we want in heaven with us, we can soften a hard heart, repel the enemy's deceptions, and receive God's answers to a seeker's questions.

Before David attacked Goliath, he told his enemy, "The battle is the Lord's." Having settled whose battle this was, "David ran quickly toward the battle line to meet him" (1 Samuel 17:47–48). That is the winning combination for God's champions today: trusting this battle totally to the Lord, then running confidently into the fight for a dying person's soul. And that means, in part, being prepared to answer the objections and remove the obstacles that can stand between a person and heaven.

There are four rescue obstacles that probably top the "All-Time Favorites" list. Because of satanic deceptions that permeate our world, they are issues that are raised over and over again as believers tell about Jesus. They are real obstacles—but the good news is that they can be overcome. You can claim the promise of Jesus on behalf of people you want in heaven with you: "You will know the truth, and the truth will set you free" (John 8:32).

ROADBLOCK ONE:
OVERCOMING "HYPOCRITES"

If I had to nominate one unbelievers' objection to the Gospel as number one, this would probably be it. There is hardly a believer that has ever tried to present Christ who has not heard someone respond, "Yeah, but what about all those hypocrites who call themselves Christians!" Sometimes the seeker is even willing to name one or two of those hypocrites for you, especially if it's a Christian leader.

Many an unbeliever has stumbled over the failures of believers on his or her road to Jesus. It is a sobering reminder that we are God's "letter . . . known and read by everybody" (2 Corinthians 3:2). We must continue to allow Christ to line up our behavior with our beliefs, lest "God's name [be] blasphemed among the Gentiles [the unreached] because of you" (Romans 2:24).

But the fact that an unbeliever is bothered by hypocrites is not a valid reason for rejecting Christ. I am so grateful that the invitation of Jesus throughout the Gospels is "Follow Me." He did not say, "Follow My followers" or "Follow My leaders" or "Follow My religion"—He said, "Follow *Me*." In fact . . .

THIS IS ALL
ABOUT *JESUS*.

The only reason not to follow Jesus is if you have a problem with Jesus. *He* is the issue! This is about a personal relationship between a pardoned sinner and a Savior who died for him.

So, if a seeker objects to the Good News because of hypocrites, then the relevant question is, "Was *Jesus* a hypocrite?" If not, then there is no reason not to belong to Him. And history records that not even Jesus' enemies could find one inconsistency between His teachings and His actions. In fact, they told Him, "We know you are a man of integrity" (Mark 12:14). Peter, who was with Jesus day in and day out, in public and in private, said, "He committed no sin, and no deceit was found in his mouth" (1 Peter 2:22).

Unfortunately, Jesus' followers are "works in progress." They have lives that are better than they were before they knew Christ, but not as good as they will be after more years with Christ. And Jesus made it clear that there would be "weeds" growing right next to the "wheat" in His church—people who apparently believe the same beliefs and look and sound like Christians, some of whom are for real and some who don't really know Him. The "hypocrite" a seeker is stumbling over may be one of those people who Jesus said "honor me with their lips, but their hearts are far from me" (Mark 7:6).

On occasion, I have turned the "hypocrite" objection into another reason for a seeker to choose Christ. I have simply said, "I'm glad you are sensitive to the inconsistencies between what Jesus taught and how some of us live. You obviously know some of what it means to belong to Jesus, so I believe you would make a great Jesus-follower!"

Any discussion of Christians or Christianity is ultimately a detour from the main road to eternal life. No one's eternity will ever be determined by what they decide about Christians or Christianity. But heaven or hell hangs on what a person decides about Jesus. "Whoever believes in *the Son* has eternal life, but whoever rejects *the Son* will not see life, for God's wrath remains on him" (John 3:36, italics added). Keep bringing the conversation back to Jesus.

ROADBLOCK TWO: "RELIGION"

When Jesus began to get close to the real issues in the life of the Samaritan woman at the well, she immediately started talking about her religion. She was not the first person or the last to use her religion as a way to dodge the Gospel. In fact, you can probably think of someone right now who is being kept from Jesus by a reliance on his or her religion. The person says, "Yes, but I'm a good Baptist ... I'm a good Catholic ... I'm a good Jew ... I'm a good Muslim." Satan is the blinder from hell; he loves to use a person's religious affiliation or the individual's personal goodness to blind him or her to the need for a personal Savior.

Unfortunately, you cannot pay a death penalty by being a good person. The Bible says that "the wages of sin is death" and that every human being is a sinner: "There is no one righteous, not even one. . . . For all have sinned and fall short of the glory of God" (Romans 6:23; 3:10, 23).

There is only one way a death penalty can be paid—somebody has to die. And Somebody did. "God demonstrates his own love for us in this: While we were still sinners, Christ died for us" (Romans 5:8). "God so loved the world that he gave his one and only Son" (John 3:16) to pay the death penalty we deserve. Our only hope is to put our total trust in the One who did the dying for the sinning we've done.

Since our going to heaven is all about what Jesus did rather than what we do, it should come as no surprise that the Bible bluntly announces that it is "not by works" (Ephesians 2:9). Those three words are as radical and revolutionary as any ever spoken in human history. They go right to the core of every religion on earth and remove the reason most people practice their religion—to do enough good to take care of the bad.

You can remind your friend who stands behind the roadblock of religion that no court in the land will accept good as a payment for bad. Let's say that I have to appear in court after a police officer gives me a traffic ticket for exceeding the speed limit. The judge then sentences me to pay a steep fine. I respond in this way: "But, your honor, I don't have to pay that fine." Considering also nailing me for contempt of court, the judge wants to know why.

"It's simple," I tell him. "The last fifty times I went through that speed zone, I kept the speed limit. So I don't have to pay for the time I didn't, right?"

This is not a recommended response. The times I've kept the law in no way cancel out the time I have broken the law.

The Judge of all mankind governs in the same way. Except His Book indicates that we have broken His laws far more times than we have kept them. And no matter how good we have been, our good cannot pay for our sin and its eternal death penalty. There is only one way to be saved from that penalty: "It is by grace [undeserved love] you have been saved, through faith—and this is not from yourselves, it is the gift of God—not by works" (Ephesians 2:8–9). A gift, by its very nature, cannot be earned; and eternal life is "the gift of God" (Romans 6:23). So a person's religion, a person's goodness, is ultimately a nonissue in whether or not they have the relationship they were created for, whether or not they will go to heaven when they die.

When the Samaritan woman tried to turn a conversation about her and Jesus into a discussion of religion, Jesus brought it right back to the central issue—our personal relationship with our Creator. Every spiritual rescuer needs to follow the Master's example.

ROADBLOCK THREE:
BITTERNESS TOWARD GOD

Jerry was on a commuter train not long ago and got involved in conversation with Lori, a student from an Ivy League university. The conversation took an unexpected turn toward the spiritual when Lori brought up the reason for being in the area. "My former roommate lives here, and she just discovered she has breast cancer. I wanted to be with her.

"She keeps saying, 'It's OK,'" Lori added. "'God is really giving me peace through all this.'" This bright young woman had indicated earlier that her own philosophy of life was totally postmodern; she believed morality was relative and had a naturalistic view of life. Lori did not have a "file folder" for the kind of personal God-relationship her friend was leaning on. But when Jerry began trying to expand the discussion about spiritual things, Lori dismissed it by saying, "I really don't have any interest in God." Jerry might have assumed the student was simply an intellectual skeptic until the woman explained her reason for considering "God" a closed subject.

"I prayed to God once—for my grandmother. But she died anyway. So He must not be there, or He must not care."

The words of that student reveal what many an unbeliever's real reason is for not believing: They are hurt or angry or bitter toward God because of something "bad" that happened. In fact, I suspect that there are relatively few people who are atheists or agnostics for mostly intellectual reasons (although those are the reasons they will cite). They are ultimately unbelievers for emotional reasons, because of something painful in their lives that they blame God for. The death of a loved one, a terrible accident, a natural disaster—and the doubter often concludes, "He must not be there, or He must not care." So as you and I ask the lost to put their trust in Jesus Christ to be their sin-Rescuer, the old feelings of "Why did God . . .?" stand in the way.

Thankfully, we are not God's defense attorneys, nor will our attempts to theologically explain away those events heal the very deep feelings of hurt and bitterness. But there are a few insights God gives us in the Bible that provide some of the "rest of the story" about life's tragedies. And they offer hope to a bitter, questioning heart.

First, God established how many years we would be on earth from the time of our conception. I recently spoke at the heartrending funeral of a precious eight-year-old boy who had died in an automobile accident. The spoken or unspoken question on everybody's heart was . . .

"WHY HIM? WHY SO SOON?"

I shared God's perspective on this boy's life from David's prayer in Psalm 139. "You created my inmost being; you knit me together in my mother's womb. . . . All the days ordained for me were written in your book before one of them came to be" (verses 13, 16).

Every person stays on earth until our work is done, and our Creator decides when that is. No matter how old a loved one is when he or she dies, it's always "too soon." But this boy's work was done in eight years, just as God planned. My baby brother's work was done in only six months—the grief over his death brought our whole family to Christ. My wife's grandmother's work took ninety-nine years. But we get all the days "ordained" for us before we have lived our first day.

When we focus on how a loved one's days ended—the cancer, the accident, the heart attack—we compound our grief. When God didn't answer that university student's prayer by healing her grandmother, it wasn't that He isn't there or doesn't care. There is a plan that was in place for Grandma's work on earth—and no matter when the last day came, it was going to hurt. But when we give God an ultimatum to "do what I say or I won't believe in You," we are unintentionally trying to reverse what "God" means. After all, the creature doesn't tell the Creator what to do. It's the other way around.

Second, God's perspective helps us by revealing that death was not part of the plan. God says that death "entered the world . . . through sin, and . . . death came to all men, because all sinned" (Romans 5:12). In fact . . .

MUCH OF THE SUFFERING IN THE WORLD THAT GOD IS BLAMED FOR IS THE RESULT OF PEOPLE DOING THE OPPOSITE OF WHAT GOD SAYS.

In addition, the penalty of death, both physical and spiritual (along with all the grief and suffering that goes with it), entered the world, not because God wanted us to die, but because we didn't want God. And if God didn't care, He could have just left us separated from Him with physical death as the end of our existence. But because "God so loved the world," He gave His only Son to reverse the eternal effect of sin, so that death is, for those who have accepted the gift of eternal life, the beginning, not the end.

Through the Bible, God also tells us this about life's hurting times: "God is our refuge and strength, an ever present help in trouble. . . . He heals the brokenhearted and binds up their wounds" (Psalm 46:1; 147:3). In fact, the Bible says of Jesus, "The Lord . . . has sent me to bind up the brokenhearted" (Isaiah 61:1). God cares deeply about the hurt in our hearts. He wants to move in close, give us supernatural strength to bear the burden (like Lori's friend who was facing cancer with God's peace), and begin to heal our broken heart. But because we so often make the mistake of turning *from God* instead of *to God* in times of tragedy, we carry the burden alone—by our choice. When we jettison God in our hurting time because we don't understand His ways, we turn our backs on the only One who offers any hope, any meaning, any healing in the hurt.

When someone we are telling about Christ is held back by a bitterness toward God, we also need to help the person understand that *Jesus identified with all the agony of all our lives when He hung on the cross.* This Savior we ask a person to trust is not a distant, unfeeling deity. Instead, when He suffered and died, "He took up our infirmities and carried our sorrows" (Isaiah 53:4). All the garbage of all the sins of all the centuries was dumped on God's Son. "He was pierced for our transgressions, he was crushed for our iniquities . . . and by his wounds we are healed" (Isaiah 53:5). This is a wounded Savior who asks us to put our trust in Him.

Ultimately, our struggles with "Is God there? Does He care?" can be answered only at the foot of Jesus' cross. And that is where we want to bring every person we hope to rescue spiritually.

ROADBLOCK FOUR:
"ALL ROADS LEAD TO GOD"

In a pluralistic society, the idea that Jesus is the only way to God seems arrogant and intolerant. Many seekers stumble over Jesus' claim to be "the way and the truth and the life" and that "no one comes to the Father except through me" (John 14:6). The Good News can sound like an arrogant putdown of all the world's great religions and the people who follow them with great sincerity. "What about the Muslims? What about the Jews? What about the Buddhists? Do you mean to tell me that they're all going to hell just because they don't believe in Jesus?" Those are the kinds of objections that can make an unbeliever stumble on his way to Jesus.

Once again, though, the Good News is not about religion, including Christianity. This isn't about one religion being better than all the other religions. The lifesaving message you have been trusted to deliver is about a *Savior* from our sin, not a *religion* to pay off our sin.

If a religion or a moral code is what we need to get the wall down between us and God, then take your pick; there are many religious systems of human goodness. But none can solve our real problem with God: the sentence of death for having run our own lives. A death penalty can only be paid by someone dying. Remember, God has described our spiritual condition as being "dead in your transgressions and sins," and He says that "when we were still powerless, Christ died for the ungodly" (Ephesians 2:1; Romans 5:6).

When I was ten years old, I almost drowned in Lake Michigan. I had gone out into the lake with my friends, too proud to tell them I didn't know how to swim. I went out farther than I should, lost my footing, and started to go under. I can still remember the panic of those awful moments as I thrashed around helplessly, watching the water close over my head and taking on water fast. My friends did nothing, thinking I was just clowning around. I was about to go down for the last time when suddenly I saw a hand reaching out to me—and I grabbed it in desperation. Obviously, that rescuer is why I lived to tell about it.

Suppose someone had rowed up to me as I was going under and thrown me a book entitled *How to Swim.* As good as those swimming instructions might have been, they would not have saved me. I was powerless to save myself. My only hope of escaping death and getting to shore was a rescuer—a savior. And a person's only hope of escaping the death penalty of his sin and getting to heaven is the Rescuer who came from heaven to save us—at the cost of His own life. No swimming instructions can save us—no Protestant swimming instructions, no Catholic swimming instructions, no Jewish swimming instructions, no Muslim, Buddhist, or Hindu swimming instructions. We are drowning spiritually!

Yes, there are many religions, many teachers, and many moral codes, but there's only one Savior. No one else even claimed to pay the death penalty for our sins. But the Bible indicates that was Jesus' mission: "There is . . . one mediator between God and men, the man Christ Jesus, who gave himself as a ransom for all men" (1 Timothy 2:5). A "ransom," of course, is the price that has to be paid to get someone back. And no one else ever walked out of a grave under his own power after he died.

EVERY LEADER OF EVERY
GREAT RELIGION IS IN
HIS GRAVE, EXCEPT ONE.

According to the testimony of six historians, Jesus Christ rose from the dead!

The message you've been given to deliver is not about Christianity being the one true religion. It's about Jesus being the only Savior from the death penalty of our sins.

As you seek to introduce Him to someone He died for, remember that you are engaging in a battle for someone's soul, for the person's eternity. Jesus placed you where you are so you could help the people there go to heaven. But it is a battle, and the Prince of Darkness is using his clever lies, desperately trying to hold onto the person you care about. Satan wants to "steal and kill and destroy" this one you love and Jesus loves; but Jesus desires to come into the person's life through you "that [he] may have life, and have it to the full" (John 10:10).

Whatever obstacles arise in the rescue—hypocrites, religion, bitterness toward God, the idea that "all roads lead to God"—remember your mission is to *stick to Jesus*. Virtually every objection takes the focus of the conversation off Jesus and onto detours such as Christians or religions or tragedies. While you cannot ignore a person's questions, you can use them to turn the conversation back to Jesus. When you do, you are foiling the enemy's central strategy for keeping a person forever—keeping them from Jesus and His cross. When you avoid all detours and take someone you care about to Jesus and His cross, you have brought them face to face with One who is your message.

NO CHEAP RESCUES

The spiritual rescue mission to which Jesus has summoned you is not without its struggles and not without its price. You may face the bullets of hostility. You may have to remove the obstacles of honest objections or questions. You may need to dig through a lot of emotional and spiritual rubble to get to the heart of someone you want in heaven with you. Rescues have never come easy. Just ask Jesus.

The great nineteenth-century gospel singer and composer Ira Sankey captured the price heaven's Rescuer paid in these moving words of the hymn he often sang, "The Ninety and Nine."

There were ninety and nine that safely lay
In the shelter of the fold,

But one was out on the hills away,
Far off from the gates of gold—
Away on the mountains wild and bare;
Away from the tender Shepherd's care.

"Lord, Thou hast here Thy ninety and nine;
Are they not enough for Thee?"
But the Shepherd made answer,
"This of Mine has wandered away from Me,
And, although the road be rough and steep,
I go to the desert to find My sheep."

But none of the ransomed ever knew
How deep were the waters crossed;
Nor how dark was the night that the Lord passed through
Ere He found His sheep that was lost.
Out in the desert He heard the cry—
Sick and helpless and ready to die. . . .

But all through the mountains thunder riven,
And up from the rocky steep,
There arose a glad cry to the gates of heaven,
"Rejoice! I have found My sheep!"
And the angels echoed around the throne,
"Rejoice, for the Lord brings back His own!"[2]

As Jesus came looking for you and me, literally nothing could stop this loving Shepherd. He laid down His life for His sheep. His was the most expensive, most important rescue in all human history.

And now He has entrusted you with the spiritual rescue of someone you care about. By God's grace, you can do whatever it takes to complete the rescue. Because lives are at stake—forever.

15
WHEN YOU'RE TRUSTED WITH A CADILLAC

"WE LOVED YOU SO MUCH THAT WE WERE DELIGHTED
TO SHARE WITH YOU NOT ONLY THE GOSPEL OF GOD
BUT OUR LIVES AS WELL ... FOR WHAT IS OUR HOPE,
OUR JOY, OR THE CROWN IN WHICH WE WILL
GLORY IN THE PRESENCE OF OUR LORD JESUS ... ?
IS IT NOT YOU? INDEED, YOU ARE OUR GLORY AND JOY."
⁓1 THESSALONIANS 2:8, 19–20⁓

Years ago I was driving along with my family, headed home from a Christmas party. All of a sudden our car came to an abrupt stop, the hood of the car bent in half, and my children started crying fearfully in the backseat. A drunk driver had suddenly crossed the center line and plowed into our car. Thankfully, none of us was seriously injured, but our vehicle went to "car heaven."

But we still needed a car, desperately, during this special Christmas season. And just as Karen and I were discussing renting one, the phone rang. A friend I'll call Daniel was offering us one of his cars for the next six weeks while he was in Florida. I gratefully accepted his offer, not knowing what kind of vehicle he would be delivering. Within the hour, Daniel drove up in his brand-new, fully equipped Cadillac Coupe deVille!

This was good news and bad news. The good news: I had a wonderful car to drive for the busy weeks ahead. The bad news: I would be responsible for someone else's brand-new luxury car.

Never has any car I've driven been so well treated. The kids knew there would not be so much as one french fry in that vehicle. I became a sudden convert to the slow lane. I considered changing the oil after every gas fill-up. Nothing has ever improved my driving so dramatically as six weeks in my friend's new Cadillac. After all, when you've been trusted with something valuable, you handle it with care.

NEWBORN CARE

That is what makes our care for one of God's newborn "babies" so vitally important. God has nothing more valuable to trust to His followers than a new believer in His Son. And as you have the unparalleled thrill of helping a person be born into God's family, you step into a priceless trust from God, the privilege of providing "newborn care" for this one who has just begun life's most important relationship. Whenever you are involved with a new member of God's family, you have been trusted by God with a "Cadillac." This baby is valuable; handle him or her with care!

I will never forget the wonderful night that our first grandchild arrived. Karen and I were in the delivery room only minutes after Jordan made his appearance. His daddy had been holding that precious little guy, but then he placed him gently in my arms. Holding the first arrival of the next generation was a moment so full of emotion that it was literally indescribable. I held that baby as carefully as I knew how— he was very valuable yet very fragile, and his father had entrusted him to me. When God allows you the privilege of being involved with Him in the birthing of a new child into His family, it is as if He places that fragile spiritual baby into your hands to hold and care for. His new child is a priceless trust.

Just as you were divinely positioned to rescue someone you care about, you are also in the best possible position to care for the person after he or she has been rescued. Typically, we think of the church as the environment for following up a new believer and a pastor as the best person to do it. There is no question that a biblical church is designed by God to be the lifelong home of a follower of Jesus Christ. But in a post-Christian culture, or even in dealing with someone from "another religious group," it may not be effective to start our newborn care by saying, "Now that you have begun your relationship with Jesus, start coming to our church."

Remember, we have just told them that this is all about a relationship, not all about a religion. If we follow their commitment with an immediate emphasis on coming to church, that can seem confusing and contradictory. After most crusades and outreaches, "follow-up" has traditionally meant referring commitment names to local churches that then are to try to get those people to their church. Historically that approach has had less than satisfying results. Part of that may be because many pre-Christian, post-Christian, or "other religion" people are not suddenly ready to become church people just because they opened their hearts to Jesus. Just as they needed a believer like you to be a bridge to Jesus, so they also may need someone like you to be a bridge to the church.

Our approach to caring for the new believer must be consistent with our approach to reaching them in the first place: connecting with them in their world, counting on a believer in their world to be the primary messenger of God's message to them, and communicating Christ to them in a place where they feel safe and in a language they understand. While the follow-up of a new member of God's family should end in a biblical church, it will probably be most effective if it begins in a nonreligious setting, guided by the "everyday Christian" who brought them to Christ. Just as modern lost people are best birthed nonreligiously, their immediate postnatal care is best carried out nonreligiously. Thus . . .

THE PRIMARY RESPONSIBILITY FOR THE CARE OF SOMEONE WHO HAS JUST BEEN BORN INTO GOD'S FAMILY RESTS WITH THE PERSON GOD USED TO HELP "DELIVER THE BABY."

If God has used you in that life-giving way, then you have not only the responsibility, but the high privilege of introducing your new spiritual brother or sister to what they got when they got Jesus.

Tragically, too many spiritual new arrivals have been left on the delivery table to fend for themselves. Often we work and pray so hard to bring people to Christ that we tend to feel "it's over" when they come to Christ. But, in reality, it's only the beginning. No one knows that better than Satan, who fought so hard to "blind" (2 Corinthians 4:4) and "steal" (John 10:10) in order to keep that person away from Jesus. Having lost that battle when a lost one comes to the Cross, he immediately tries to attack their new relationship with Christ.

In fact, Jesus said that as soon as people hear the word, "Satan comes and takes away the word that was sown in them" (Mark 4:15). Never is a human more vulnerable, more easily infected than right after he or she has been born. That's why hospital workers take such elaborate precautions with a newborn baby. Similarly, the devil tries to move in quickly to undermine a person's fragile new commitment to Jesus Christ. So Satan believes in immediate follow-up! If *we* don't believe in immediate follow-up, we allow the enemy's lies and questions to come against the new believer unchallenged.

In Jesus' words, "I chose you to go and bear fruit—fruit that will *last*" (John 15:16, italics added). If God has used you to help a lost loved one enter God's family, then you have fulfilled that divine destiny to "bear fruit." Now your care for God's new baby will play a decisive part in whether or not your fruit "will last."

BECOMING A PEDIATRICIAN

When you help someone you care about "receive Him" and become a "child of God" (John 1:12), you have, in a sense, served as a spiritual obstetrician, delivering a baby into God's family. At that point, your mission changes to that of a spiritual pediatrician, helping this newborn get off to a strong and healthy start in Christ. Just as the experiences of a child in their early weeks and months shape the person they will be for the rest of their life, so a baby in God's family will be imprinted for life by what they experience—or don't experience—of their new God-relationship.

The care of a spiritual newborn begins with *fervent prayer* for your Father's new child. Paul spoke often of his frequent prayer for those he had introduced to Jesus. "In all my prayers for all of you, I always pray with joy ... being confident of this, that he who began a good work in you will carry it on to completion until the day of Christ Jesus" (Philippians 1:4, 6). Your prayers—and those of other believers you call to intercede immediately on behalf of one who has come to Christ—help to immunize this fragile new life against the enemy's guaranteed attacks.

Your pediatric care continues, as you *help the new believer* understand *and* experience *his or her new relationship with Jesus Christ*. Arrange to get together with the new believer within seventy-two hours of his or her commitment to Christ. Remind the new Christian of what he received when he prayed that heart-opening prayer. He didn't get a religion or a rulebook or some new beliefs. He got a person—he got *Jesus*. Jesus' invitation is, "Come to *me*" (Matthew 11:28, italics added), and that's what he did. It's all about Jesus. Because you faithfully gave your loved one the good news about Jesus, you now can give the new believer the great news that "you finally have the relationship you were made for, with the One you were made by!"

But how can you help a new believer understand and experience this very real, very powerful relationship with Someone he cannot see? Obviously, he needs to learn about how this relationship works, but information alone is not enough. My relationship with my wife, Karen, did not develop purely based on some attractive facts I learned about her. It came through a series of experiences with her that really brought us close. It's the same in a relationship with Christ. A new believer *needs to learn some of the wonderful facts* about their new God-relationship—but the person *also needs some experiences* with Him right away in order to make the truth come alive.

Too many times, the follow-up of a new believer is limited to information about Jesus. I call it "fill in the blank" follow-up, the kind of answers asked for in our typical follow-up materials. For instance, "Q: Who has sinned? A: All. Q: What did Jesus die for? A: Our sin." But beyond learning about this awesome new Person in their life, the spiritual beginner needs to experience how this relationship works. So as we spend intentional "postnatal care" time with God's new child, we need to ...

HELP THEM *LEARN* ABOUT JESUS *BY DOING THINGS* WITH JESUS.

Once I visited our local bakery to buy two bagels. As I placed my order, the bakery lady asked me if I would like some cheesecake. Before I could answer, she spoke two of my favorite words: "It's free." The bakers had placed little samples of their cheesecake right on top of the display case, where I could almost hear them whispering, "Taste me." So I tried the sample. Then I left the bakery with my two bagels—and a cheesecake. I hadn't planned to buy a cheesecake. But they gave me a taste of it, and then I wanted the whole thing. Give the new believer a good taste of following Christ during their early days with Him, and he will crave "the whole cheesecake."

This is what the psalmist calls "tasting" of the Lord. The Bible instructs us to "taste and see that the Lord is good" (Psalm 34:8). In the early days and weeks of a new believer's relationship with Jesus, he needs to get some "tastes" of what he needs to be doing with Him for the rest of his life. If the new believer gets a good taste of following Christ in his first days with Him, he probably will want much more.

So as we introduce God's precious newborns to their new Savior, it is important to give them not only the truth, but the truth with projects. Pediatric care often includes special projects for the newborn believers. They need to learn some aspect of how to relate to Jesus and then have a short-term project in which they *do* what they learned. After that, they have an opportunity to come back and talk with their spiritual pediatrician about how it went.

Thus the early weeks of a new believer's life in Christ should be a series of experiences that follow this cycle:

LEARN IT . . .
DO IT . . .
TALK ABOUT IT.

First, they *learn* one of the basics about their new Jesus-relationship. Then, for the next few days, they have a spiritual project in which they *do* what they learned. That's followed by a debriefing where they *talk about* what happened when they did what they learned. They are immediately integrating their new relationship into real life, and you are carrying out your Lord's prime directive to "make disciples . . . , teaching them to obey everything I have commanded you" (Matthew 28:19–20).

EXPERIENCING THE FIVE SECRETS
OF A GREAT RELATIONSHIP WITH GOD

Just as we reach people by speaking the language they understand, we should follow up in their words, as well. When it comes time to explain to a newly born believer how to grow in the relationship he or she just began, we dare not suddenly revert to "Christianese." It is important that we explain "where to from here" in nonreligious words. "Having devotions," "obedience," "being filled with the Spirit," or "dedicating your life" will probably be as confusing to them as being "saved" or "born again."

If the life-or-death message you delivered to your friend was about a relationship, as we noted in the previous chapter, then your after-rebirth message should also be about a relationship. You showed this one you care about how to begin life's most important relationship; now you have the honor of showing her how to make this new relationship a great relationship—how just as she "received Christ Jesus as Lord," she can "continue to live in him, rooted and built up in him" (Colossians 2:6–7).

How can the basics of belonging to Jesus be explained to your new spiritual brother or sister in everyday language? And how can you help

189

them experience those basics, not just learn about them? By introducing them to what I call *the five secrets of a great relationship with God!* Interestingly enough, they are elements of any great relationship and, therefore, relatively easy to grasp.

Ideally, you might introduce these by meeting with your "newborn" friend once a week over a five-week period of time. In each get-together, you would explain biblically one of the relationship secrets and then give them an "action lab" for the week, a practical project that will let them do with Jesus what they just learned. Then, the next time, you would ask them to talk about what happened when they did what they learned. In so doing, you will be starting them in that life-changing habit of *learn it . . . do it . . . talk about it.*

As we look at these five "secrets," a word of caution. If the person you rescued is of the opposite sex, give this duty to a member of the opposite sex. This will allow the new follower the freedom to discuss a fuller scope of issues and also will prevent potential misunderstanding in the discipling relationship. You can tell the new Christian, "Another woman (man) will be helping you grow, so that you can have the freedom to ask questions and interact in all areas of your life. But let's keep in touch; I want to hear how you're doing and how to pray wisely for you."

SECRET NUMBER ONE:
READ WHAT GOD HAS WRITTEN TO YOU

When I was in college, my roommate Don used to get love letters from his girlfriend. We all knew when he had received one—he was in "la-la land" all day. I noticed that he would always go off somewhere alone and read what Amy had written to him. Then he would read it again. And again. After his fifth reading or so, I wanted to say, "Don, there is no new information here!" But it wouldn't have done any good.

It was when I started to receive love letters from Karen that I began to understand. Now *I* was reading the same words over and over again! Why? Because when I was reading what she wrote to me, I was being *with* her—until I could really be with her.

It's the same way with a new believer and the Love Letter he has received from the One who loves him most—it's called the Bible. Someone who belongs to Jesus feels he is with Him as he reads what He wrote to him. This lover of Jesus continues to read regularly, until one day in heaven when he will be with his Savior forever.

That's why God tells us, "Like newborn babies, crave pure spiritual milk, so that by it you may grow up in your salvation" (1 Peter 2:2). That "spiritual milk" is "the living and enduring word of God" (1 Peter 1:23), known to us as the Bible. So in their first days in Christ, new believers should be introduced to the importance of daily reading God's Love Letter to them. We need to call their attention to the privilege of spending time with Jesus through what He wrote. This is not to be a ritualistic "Bible reading time," but time with a friend.

THE FIRST SECRET OF A GREAT GOD-RELATIONSHIP IS ABOUT TIME WITH A *PERSON*, NOT TIME WITH A *BOOK*.

As a practical matter, it is important for us to help new believers set a time and a place to meet with Jesus each new day. If we leave Him until we "get around to Him," we never will. It is fundamental to growing in this new relationship that believers set a daily date with the Person who loves them most.

It's important, too, to help God's new child know where to read in the Bible and how to read the Bible. The "where" should be a book that is easy to understand and easy to apply to your life—books such as Mark, Ephesians, James, and Proverbs. The "how" should emphasize asking oneself two questions about what he or she reads. Two primary questions would be: "In my own words, what is God saying here?" and "What am I going to do differently today because God said that?" In other words, "Do not merely listen to the word. . . . Do what it says" (James 1:22). The apostle James compares someone who takes in what God says but doesn't do anything about it to "a man who looks at his face in a mirror and, after looking at himself, goes away and immediately forgets what he looks like" (James 1:23-24). If the Bible is supposed to be a believer's mirror, then the believer can't just look into that mirror without changing something.

Once you explain the importance of reading what God has written, it is time to give God's new child an "action lab" so she can do what she just learned. So give her a notebook and ask her to write this title on the front of it: "My Times with Jesus." This will be her "Jesus Journal."

Your challenge to the new believer might go something like this: "Each day for the next week, ask God to show you something He wants you to know, then read a few verses in the book of James. It's easy to apply to your life! Read them two or three times. Then write in your Jesus Journal the date, what verses you read, and your answer to two helpful questions: 'In my own words, what is God saying here?' and 'What am I going to do differently today because He said it?'" When you get together the next time, ask the person to bring the journal so you can talk about how those times with Jesus went.

As the spiritual caregiver for this new member of God's family, you have the joy of giving the person some exciting news about her newly begun relationship. Every day, she has the same message from God that greets many Internet users when they check their E-mail: "You've got mail." In this case, it's from God Himself.

SECRET NUMBER TWO:
TALK TO GOD

Ask ten people what is the most important ingredient in making a relationship work, and most of them are likely to give the same answer: "Communication." And it is no less true in a personal relationship with God. So in the early days of belonging to Jesus, a person needs to learn how to talk with the One she has just come to know.

As you meet with a new believer, you have the privilege of introducing him or her to God's exciting invitation to His children: "Let us then approach the throne of grace with confidence, so that we may receive mercy and find grace to help us in our time of need" (Hebrews 4:16). God has invited us to come right into His presence and claim His forgiveness for our sins and His help for our needs. This is talking to God. Being in a personal conversation with God can make a powerful difference. As Paul wrote, "Do not be anxious about anything, but in everything, by prayer and petition, with thanksgiving, present your requests to God. And the peace of God, which transcends all understanding, will guard your hearts and your minds in Christ Jesus" (Philippians 4:6–7).

Having been introduced to the importance of talking to God, the new believer needs to experience communicating with Him. One possible action lab you can encourage is to write some letters to God before your next get-together. You may even want to give the person a template for his letters that includes the following:

> *Dear Lord,*
> *I love You ...*
>
> *Thank You for ...*
>
> *I'm sorry for ...*
>
> *Please ...*
>
> *Love,*

As a new child of God writes thoughts like these to their Father, he is practicing the ingredients in powerful praying. And this outline puts talking to God into the same kind of straightforward language we use in our other conversations. When you get together again, your new brother or sister can bring those letters so you can talk about how their first communications with God went.

SECRET NUMBER THREE:
BE WITH GOD'S FRIENDS

When I started dating my wife in college, I got more than one new relationship in the deal, and so did she. I got Karen's friends, and she got mine. That's the nature of any relationship; you become friends with their friends. A relationship with God is no different. In fact, the Scripture urges those who belong to Him to "not give up meeting together" so that they can "spur one another on toward love and good deeds" and "encourage one another" (Hebrews 10:24–25).

A new member of God's family should be shown in his very early days that he is not alone—that many others have been rescued from their sin by Jesus and now want to live for the One who died for them. Every believer, new and established, needs to be with those "friends of God." By doing so, each believer can (1) learn what others have learned about Him, (2) give and receive encouragement to live His way, and (3) be with others who have traveled much farther down the road some of us are just starting out on.

A simple example can underscore the importance of your new brother or sister linking up with God's friends. Have them hold their hand out in front with their fingers wide apart. Tell them to hit you (not too hard!) in the face with their fingers separated like that. Then tell them to pull those fingers tightly together in a fist. They may be anxious to try the face experiment this time, but, for survival reasons, you can stop there—you've made your point. "Which is more powerful," you ask, "separate fingers or fingers pulled together in a fist? Obviously, your fingers together. That's why God tells us to hook up with His friends: We have a lot more power together than we ever could standing alone as separate 'fingers.'"

Having explained the relationship secret of being with God's friends, you have actually helped build a bridge to the church. You have shown spiritual reasons for getting involved with God's people rather than just pouncing on them to "go to church." It's all part of a great new relationship.

The "do it, then talk about it" action lab can be to attend a church this Sunday where a personal relationship with Christ is stressed, to sit near the front, and to take notes on what is sung, prayed, and preached. Those notes should attempt to answer the same questions used in reading God's Love Letter, "What did God say to me here today?" and "What am I going to do differently this week because of it?"

SECRET NUMBER FOUR: LEARNING TO DO WHAT MAKES GOD HAPPY

There was no way our son was going to get interested in the classical music we encouraged him to explore or in the positive country music his mother liked. But then one day he picked me up at the airport with a Handel's *Messiah* cassette in the tape player and a country station occupying one of the "most listened to" buttons on his car radio. Somehow our son had suddenly developed an interest in classical music and country music. How did this happen? A *woman* happened, that's how! He was dating a music major who liked classical music because of her training and country music because of where she grew up. Isn't it amazing how we can change for someone we care about?

Again, the new believer's relationship with God is no different from any other love relationship. You want to do the things that make this Person happy, you want to stop doing the things that make this Person sad. Jesus put it this way: "If you love me, you will obey what I command" (John 14:15). One of the secrets of a great God-relationship is to begin to change things in your life based on what pleases or displeases the One who loves you most.

As God's new child reads what He's written, talks to Him, and spends time with His friends, he or she will begin to understand what brings pleasure and what brings pain to our Savior. Seeking to pursue "What would Jesus do?" we begin to experience the reality of being the "new creation" God says we are because of Christ (2 Corinthians 5:17). Our pursuit of life Jesus' way is not so much to keep from breaking religious rules as it is to keep from breaking Jesus' heart!

In order for this relationship secret to take hold, your new brother or sister needs to integrate it immediately into an action lab for the next few days. That could be something as simple as finishing this sentence on a note card: "One thing I think Jesus would like to change in me is . . ." You can then encourage the person to consciously turn over that part of her life to Jesus each new morning, asking Him to give the power to change. And, of course, have the person bring that card to your next get-together so you can talk about how this experiment in pleasing Him worked.

SECRET NUMBER FIVE:
TALK ABOUT HIM

No one has to tell a young woman to talk about her boyfriend. No one has to tell a parent to talk about his or her children—or a grandparent to talk about "the world's most beautiful grandchildren." It is natural to talk about the people you love. As a person begins a love relationship with God, he or she should know that we who love Him are "Christ's ambassadors," delivering Christ's Good News "on Christ's behalf" (2 Corinthians 5:20). We should speak about our relationship with Jesus as naturally as we do any relationship with someone who really loves us.

Converting that into an action lab for a new believer can mean teaching them that "three-open prayer" we explored earlier in this book: "Lord, open a natural opportunity for me to tell someone about my relationship with You; open their heart; open my mouth when You open the door." The project for that week can be encouraging the new believer to pray that prayer every day, expecting God to answer it and stepping up when He does. That should make for an interesting debriefing when they come to your next get-together and talk about it.

POWER IN THE BASICS

As you introduce God's new child to these secrets of having a great relationship with Him, you are giving her a taste of what you pray their whole life will be like. These simple secrets comprise the basics of following Jesus Christ, taught and experienced in the first weeks of the newborn's new life.

It is said that when the legendary football coach Vince Lombardi used to get his championship NFL teams to training camp, he spent most of his time going over how to block, how to tackle, how to hold onto the ball—the fundamentals those players must have learned when they were teenagers. But he said, "Whenever these guys blow it, they blow it on *the basics.*" If you think back over the times you have blown it spiritually, you will find that, in most cases, you blew it on one of the basics we just reviewed—one of the secrets of having a great relationship with God. Helping your new brother or sister in God's family understand and experience those basics is one of the greatest gifts you could ever give them.

You loved that person enough to take the risks to rescue them from spiritual death. Now you are loving them enough to launch them boldly into this relationship with Jesus that can change everything. And in so doing, you are loving Jesus, too. When Jesus asked Simon Peter three times, "Do you love me?" Peter answered yes each time. And Jesus responded with this simple command: "Feed my lambs" (John 21:15–17).

As Jesus turns to you with His most important question, how do you answer? "Do you love Me?" "Oh, yes, Lord, You know that I love You." Now hear His poignant response: "Then feed My lambs." If He entrusts one of His little lambs to you, you can do no less.

16
ETERNITY 9-1-1

"ROUSE THE WARRIORS! . . .
BRING DOWN YOUR WARRIORS, O LORD! . . .
SWING THE SICKLE, FOR THE HARVEST IS RIPE . . .
MULTITUDES, MULTITUDES IN THE VALLEY OF DECISION!"
⊸JOEL 3:9, 11, 13–14⊸

Oklahoma City. It is almost impossible to hear that name without thinking of the horrifying day in 1995 when the Murrah Federal Building was ripped apart by a terrorist bomb. On that deadly April 19 morning, hundreds of workers were busy in their offices, countless citizens were taking care of government business, and scores of children were playing in the building's day care center. And then, in a few wrenching moments, the building was no more. The bomb blast reduced it to a pile of shattered concrete, twisted metal, and smothering debris.

Suddenly the agenda of a city changed. Whatever had mattered before the explosion, only one thing really mattered afterward: rescue. People from many walks of life—police officers, firefighters, nurses, doctors, emergency medical technicians, construction workers, ministers, ordinary citizens who just happened to be there—dropped whatever else they were doing in order to help save whoever was still alive. Even fast-food restaurants went into emergency mode, preparing meals for the rescuers.

In what seemed only a matter of minutes, much of Oklahoma City was fully mobilized and working together on a "whatever it takes" basis. Rescuers were plunging into the dangerous rubble of that building, seemingly oblivious to the risks. The reason for this desperate, urgent, unprecedented mobilization was clear: If the rescuers got to the people trapped in that building, those people had a chance to live. If the rescuers didn't get to them, they would die there. At the end of the rescue mission, 168 people lay dead. But scores of people had been saved, thanks to the relentless work of the rescuers.

The total, selfless, fully mobilized effort to save the dying in Oklahoma City is not unique to that dark day. That kind of response is what happens whenever people realize there is a life-or-death rescue emergency. When an earthquake in Turkey levels an apartment building, when skiers are trapped in an avalanche, when a toddler is trapped in a well in Texas, the response is always the same—drop everything and pull together. That's how it is when lives depend on a total lifesaving effort.

God's rescue team, however, doesn't always see the life-and-death issue. The issue is not just giving people a few more years on earth but their *eternity* in heaven or hell. Though the Bible makes it clear that we believers are surrounded by people who are "being led away to death" (Proverbs 24:11), we often feel little sense that we have a life-or-death emergency to respond to. Thus day after day, people all around us go on dying inside and one day dying eternally, mainly because none of us went in to rescue them.

Once we sense the urgency, however, we will go into action. We need to dial Eternity 9-1-1—we need to see the emergency situation. When we see the world this way—when we see our neighbors, our friends, our coworkers through Jesus' eyes—we begin to see those around us as dying people, as those the Son of God gave His life to rescue. And, like those fully activated rescuers in Oklahoma City, we will know what we have to do; we will drop everything and go in after those whose lives are eternally at stake. If we go in to rescue them, they will have a chance to live. If we don't, they will die.

The rescue imperative begins in one heart—a heart like yours. But there are far too many people in danger for any one person to rescue alone. Rescue means a *total mobilization!* It means a rallying of God's people throughout a church, throughout a community to come together to reach as many dying people as possible. In the words of one veteran pastor when he heard I was writing this book—"Just tell me how to mobilize an *army* of believers who will care about reaching the lost!" Indeed, it is the impassioned prayer of the Son for the Father "to send out workers into his harvest field" (Matthew 9:38).

RECOGNIZING OUR MISTAKES

It is not that there are no outreach efforts in the Christian community—it's just that those outreaches are usually populated mostly by the already rescued. Few believers bring, they just come. Mobilizing God's sleeping rescuers into a passionate army is obviously a challenging goal. But the life-or-deathness of our mission demands nothing less. Most unbelievers will never have a chance at life unless and until most believers realize they are God's rescue plan.

Many efforts to mobilize on behalf of the lost are hampered by four common mistakes (two of which we have alluded to earlier in the book). If we can eliminate these mistakes that keep rescue mobilization from happening, we can begin to see the birth of that "army of believers who will care about reaching the lost."

One common mistake made by those who are planning a spiritual rescue effort is assuming the "want to." I talked to one of the leading evangelists in the world about his team's major thrust to reach one of America's great cities. Much time and money had been invested. The executive committee was a "who's who" of the area's Christian leaders; the outreach programs offered were attractive and well-promoted. Still, although there were people who came to Christ during this massive rescue effort, the results were far less than expected in light of all the work and investment.

As my evangelist friend and I talked about this disappointment, it became clear that the problem was not with the leadership, the messenger, the promotion, or the program. It boiled down to one simple, tragic reality: Even though the believers of the area had been given a special opportunity to reach their lost friends and loved ones, *they did not bring lost people to the outreaches.* As usual, God's people came, but they did not bring, for the most part. So many times, in so many places, that scenario has been repeated as a rescue apparatus is put in place, but the rescuers don't go get anyone who needs to be rescued.

If you have a heart to launch a program for reaching lost people where you are, you cannot assume that God's people have the "want to." Whether your burden is to mobilize believers for personal outreach one-on-one or public outreach through special events, literature distribution, or door-to-door efforts, it will have little impact unless believers want to have a way to rescue the dying. The chances are they neither see the people around them as spiritually dying people nor do they have any sense that they are responsible for rescuing them.

When Nehemiah, one of the Bible's great mobilizers, needed to rouse an army to rebuild his broken city, he knew it was not enough that "God had put [it] in my heart to do" (Nehemiah 2:12). It had to get into everyone else's heart! Setting a strong example for all of us who want to mobilize God's people to do God's work, he didn't start by introducing a great program; he first showed them the desperate need. Nehemiah led the community leaders on a tour of the shattered walls and gates of Jerusalem. The people saw the tragedy and their responsibility and opportunity to change it only after someone with a broken heart for the need helped them see it. (Read Nehemiah 2:13–17.) Then, and only then, did he suggest a building program, as a response to a need that had now touched the people's hearts. Their answer: "Let us start rebuilding" (Nehemiah 2:18).

Clearly . . .

RESCUE MOBILIZATION MUST BE PRECEDED BY RESCUE MOTIVATION.

It is better to assume that most believers don't have a "rescue the dying" want-to—and to take time first to help them realize what an awful thing it is to be without Christ. Such motivation must precede mobilization. They must see that God has put them in the position to save lives that will otherwise be lost.

A second mistake that contributes to an apathetic response to a rescue effort is using worn-out words. When we talk with Christians about "evangelism" or "witnessing" or "soul-winning," they don't exactly hear marching music. Generally, believers have heard words like these so much or with such negative connotations that they are immune to them. These, of course, are in-house forms of Christianese. "Evangelism" is perceived to be an institutional word. It's seen as being a church committee, a church program, something for a few spiritual "Green Berets" called "evangelists" or people "who have the gift." But few everyday Christians hear a summons to personal action on behalf of people they know when they hear a call to get involved in "evangelism."

"Witnessing" is another word that has been worn out by so much use. It's a good word, especially in light of the fact that Jesus said, "You will be my witnesses" (Acts 1:8). But unfortunately it is often not a motivating word when it comes to mobilizing believers to join in an effort to reach the lost. "Witnessing" often sounds like a predictable entry on the oft-repeated litany of "my Christian duties," right after "Bible reading and prayer." It is also associated by many either with a church program or with an intrusive, pushy approach to trying to "win a soul," something most believers do not feel is for them.

That is why I have virtually replaced some of these good but worn-out words with the idea of *rescue*. Calling people to spiritual rescue conveys the urgency, the passion, the "life-or-deathness" of what Jesus is summoning His followers to do. As we try to rally our fellow believers to do something about the dying people around them, we must not let our efforts falter because we used words that are too flat and familiar to ignite a spiritual fire.

A third common mistake in planning a spiritual rescue effort is defending our turf. The rescue army of God tends to remain split up into little "kingdoms," separated by denomination, worship styles, jealousies, fear of losing, and theological differences, usually over issues that are unrelated to our rescue message of Christ's death for our sins. One can only imagine the tragedy if, on the day of the Oklahoma City explosion, the separate agencies had refused to work together because of their "turfs."

A few years ago the New York news reported that a helicopter had crashed into the East River with several tourists aboard. Almost immediately, three scuba divers were on the scene from one city agency. With people trapped in the chopper at the bottom of the river, they went right to work to find them. Right away, nine more divers arrived from another city agency. I remember vividly the report of what happened next: The additional divers were stopped at the dock by an officer in the first agency. He forbade those nine divers from entering the water because "we were here first and we've got it covered."

Tragically, one tourist died at the bottom of the East River that day—not so much because of the crash, but because the people who could have rescued him were arguing over turf!

For emergency rescuers and the people of God, the truth is the same . . .

TURF DOESN'T MATTER WHEN PEOPLE ARE DYING!

We are so afraid of losing some people in our group when we should be concerned much more about losing people outside all our groups for all eternity! Or we are focused on who will get the credit for the rescue when all that really matters is that the dying people get rescued.

When the apostle Paul called us to live "in a manner worthy of the gospel of Christ," he described that worthy way: "Stand firm in one spirit, contending as one man for the faith of the gospel" (Philippians 1:27). "Worthy of the gospel" means battling for Christ as *one* unit, not many. Anything else is *un*worthy of the message God has committed to us.

A united rescue effort means much more than your group planning an outreach and then inviting all the other groups to come and help populate it. It means conceiving your rescue strategy *together* and praying for the lost *together*. It includes sharing the leadership, meeting on neutral ground (not "your place" or "my place"), and mobilizing *all* of God's people for the effort. Like the "all hands" effort to save lives after the Oklahoma City bombing, people's lives—people's *forevers*—depend on whether or not God's rescuers work together.

The fourth common mistake in planning a spiritual rescue effort is having programs without prayer. No mistake undermines that mobilization more.

One reason the first Christians made such a powerful impact on their city was because "all the believers were together . . . and the Lord added to their number daily those who were being saved" (Acts 2:44, 47). Study the widely varied backgrounds and the competitiveness of the disciples, and it will become clear that a united effort had to be a work of God. It always is. Before any of those thousands of people were won to Christ, the believers had "joined together constantly in prayer" (Acts 1:14).

BEFORE GOD'S PEOPLE CAN REALLY *WORK* TOGETHER, THEY NEED TO *PRAY* TOGETHER.

It is not a combined outreach effort that will unite God's divided army—it is combined *praying* for the lost and dying people all around them, and for the broken heart of Jesus over those He died for. When Baptists and Pentecostals and Presbyterians and mainline folks and parachurch leaders agonize together on their knees for those who are "without hope and without God in the world" (Ephesians 2:12), you can almost feel the walls coming down and the hearts coming together. The miraculous rescue unity of Jesus' first followers was ultimately an answer to His prayer for them to "be brought to complete unity to let the world know that you sent me" (John 17:23). Two thousands years later, the story is still the same.

GIVING EVERY DYING PERSON A CHANCE

It was my father's last visit to the hospital. He would not recover from the open-heart surgery that awaited him in a few days. But he had, as it turned out, one last mission to carry out for his Lord. And that mission's name was Andy.

Andy was my dad's hospital roommate in those days leading up to the surgery. My father, John Hutchcraft, would never have considered himself a preacher, an evangelist, or even a "great Christian" (although *I* consider him a great Christian!), but he did see people like his roommate through the eyes of Jesus. When he discovered that Andy had never begun a personal relationship with Jesus Christ, Dad knew he had been given a rescue assignment from God. So, in his own humble way, my father told his roommate about the Savior who had changed his life. And before my dad went to the surgery that would ultimately bring him into Jesus' arms, Andy gave his heart to Christ. Although it meant missing work and driving a distance, Andy was at my father's funeral to pay tribute to the man who had given him Jesus.

As far as I know, Andy had never had a chance to find eternal life. How did he get his chance? Not from being in a church, attending a crusade, or hearing from a skilled evangelist. Andy will be in heaven someday because an everyday Christian named John understood who he was and why he was where he was: He was Jesus' designated rescuer, placed in a particular hospital room to introduce the roommate he found there to his Savior.

If you multiply that eternal drama millions of times over to include every Jesus-follower and the lost people in their world, you can begin to see a picture of how so many more dying people can go to heaven instead of hell. The simple equation of giving every person a chance at the life Jesus died to give them comes down to this:

EVERY BELIEVER
A RESCUER
EQUALS EVERY DYING
PERSON A CHANCE.

Unless each everyday believer sees the rescue of the people in their circle of influence as his and her personal responsibility, most lost people will go on living and dying without Jesus. In spite of all our Christian radio programs, TV programs, and evangelistic programs, most dying people will never be touched by them. If we think someone else is going to reach our friends, then our friends will probably just go on dying.

In reality, most unbelievers have a believer living close by their world. If every believer saw himself as God does—uniquely positioned by Him to give those people a chance at heaven—then countless unreached men and women could finally meet the God-man who died for them.

CALLING ALL LIFEGUARDS

I read recently about a growing "lifeguard shortage" at many of America's beaches. Such a shortage, of course, must be addressed aggressively because unguarded beaches eventually mean lives lost. Similarly, the spiritual "beaches" of your community are supposed to have lifeguards. Jesus has assigned His followers to look after the people around them. But many of His lifeguards either cannot see that people they know are spiritually dying or they don't see that the rescue is up to them.

Perhaps you have answered the summons of Jesus to join Him in His rescue mission. Now you can get many other believers to join Him, too. Here are five motivating steps.

Your first step in encouraging every believer to be a rescuer is *to pray for a wake-up call from God*. Jesus told us we would have to "ask the Lord of the harvest . . . to send out workers into his harvest" (Matthew 9:38). The Greek word translated "send out" carries the sense of "forcible expelling." Only God can pick up the workers and throw them out into the harvest. The battle to get God's people into the harvest must be fought primarily and passionately on your knees. A broken heart for the lost is nothing less than a miraculous work of Almighty God.

The second step in motivating believers to become rescuers is to *encourage them to have a burden for someone specific*. This can begin by asking Christians you know, "What lost person are you going to look for when you get to heaven? Whom will you ask Jesus about there? 'Lord, is _____ here?' What if Jesus answers, "Oh, did you bring him? Did you bring her?'" A Christian will never throw himself or herself into spiritual rescue so long as "lost" is just a faceless group of people or a theological concept. "Lost" needs a name! Our mission is to help them begin their lifesaving work by owning one lost friend or loved one as their spiritual responsibility.

One of the very first men to follow Jesus, Andrew, demonstrated the power of a focused burden—"Andrew, Simon Peter's brother, . . . followed Jesus. The first thing Andrew did was to find his brother Simon and tell him, 'We have found the Messiah.' . . . Then he brought Simon to Jesus" (John 1:40–42).

A third step in solving the critical "lifeguard shortage" is to *introduce believers to their assignment as Christ's ambassador to their personal "tribe."* Once you realize that what you do at work or school or in your neighborhood is really just your "clever disguise" for bringing Jesus into people's lives, you can help others see how God has positioned them.

A fourth step in motivating believers to become rescuers is to *provide a practical way of presenting the Gospel.* As we have trained thousands in the simple "relationship Gospel" explained in an earlier chapter—(1) "There's a relationship you're created to have . . . (2) you don't have, (3) you can have, and (4) you must choose"—many have said, "Now I can do *that!*" Once believers have the want-to, they need a simple how-to. When you equip them with that, you have emboldened them to "not (be) ashamed of the gospel" (Romans 1:16).

The final step is to *provide rescue opportunities they can trust.* Once believers begin to develop their Lord's heart for dying people, they need outreach events that can help them bring their friends under the hearing of Jesus' good news. Tragically, the history of many harvest events is that they are populated mostly by those already rescued, usually because not many believers bring unbelievers.

That brings us to an all-important equation for having a spiritual harvest. The harvest equation reads:

Trust + bring someone = harvest

There won't be much of a harvest if Christians don't bring the lost to the outreach. And there won't be much bringing unless the Christians trust what they're bringing their lost friends to. Many Christians, knowing that they may only get one shot to give their friend the Good News, don't want to risk this relationship on something that might backfire spiritually. So it is up to those of us who are mobilizing a rescue team to provide outreach opportunities that will be appealing and understandable to the people they are supposed to reach.

In an increasingly post-Christian world, it is going to be more and more difficult to get a lost person to a religious place to hear a religious speaker talk about a religious subject. A rescue event is most effective when it has four characteristics:

1. It is in a setting where lost people feel comfortable.
2. It is with people around whom they feel comfortable.
3. It deals with a subject they care about.
4. It is in a language they can understand.

When my surgeon friend wanted his professional friends and colleagues to hear the good news about Jesus, he held a dinner at a country club (a setting where they felt comfortable) . . . for business and professional people (people around whom they felt comfortable) . . . asking me to speak about "Peaceful Living in a Stressful World" (a subject they cared about) . . . counting on me to present Jesus without "Christianese" (in a language they could understand). The country club was packed with unbelievers, and "unlikely candidates" met Jesus.

When the new pastor of our church wanted to reach the lost, he asked Christian couples to invite their lost neighbors to their home for an "Ask any spiritual question you want" discussion with "Pastor Earl." The place (a living room) and the people (folks from the neighborhood) felt comfortable; they got to talk about things they wanted to know; and our pastor came casual, without "Christianese," and called himself by his first name. One of the strongest churches in our area was built on the fruits of those powerful living-room outreaches.

When we put the life saving message of Jesus in a nonreligious, seeker-sensitive package, we empower His followers with important rescue tools. We help them take someone they love to heaven with them.

God's plan for saving a dying world rests upon the obedience of those who have been rescued by His Son. Once they are the rescued, He expects them to become rescuers of other dying people. Indeed, Jesus told His followers, "As the Father has sent me, I am sending you" (John 20:20). Once we have answered His call to greatness—His summons to His life-saving work—we must urge our fellow believers to "open your eyes and look at the fields! They are ripe for harvest" (John 4:35). An *army* of rescuers is desperately needed to fulfill God's eternal plan for spreading the Jesus-fire. As King David wrote, "The Lord announced the word, and great was the company of those who proclaimed it" (Psalm 68:11).

"I COULD HARVEST IT ALL . . ."

Our son Doug had just arrived on the mission field to which God had called him—an Indian reservation in the Southwest. And in trying to make some connections with his new neighbors, he offered to help a tribal leader in his cornfield.

That sounds simple enough, except for some complicating factors: On this semi-arid reservation, it is very challenging to grow corn; every stalk is precious. In addition, corn is considered sacred. The greatest problem, Doug found, was as a suburban boy he had no idea what he was doing in a cornfield. So when the tribal leader asked this new missionary to hoe his cornfield, it was, to say the least, a challenging assignment. But Doug rose to the challenge, although fearing all day that he would be chopping down sacred corn with those nasty weeds.

Apparently, the missionary rookie did not do too much damage; the tribal leader honored him by inviting him to stay for dinner. As they ate, the native man said, "You know, I'll end up being able to harvest only about 10 percent of my corn crop." Doug was shocked to hear that. "Is that because there's so little rain?" he asked. He has never forgotten his host's reply: "No. It's because I can't find enough people to help me bring in the harvest. *I could harvest it all if I could only find enough workers.*"

Jesus knows that feeling. He could harvest so many more lives if only He could find enough workers. He has found you. Now—because you cannot let more people die without a chance—help Jesus find some more.

Epilogue
TURNING THE LIFEBOATS AROUND

There is a legend told concerning the return of Jesus to heaven. Behind the legend is an eternal truth worth considering. Indeed, the truth can forever change what you live for.

As Gabriel welcomed the Son of God back to His heavenly home some two thousand years ago, Jesus repeated the words He had spoken in His final moments on the cross: "It is finished!" Christ went on to explain that His divinely appointed lifesaving mission had been completed.

While Gabriel rejoiced with the Master over His "mission accomplished," he did have some questions. "Now how will the world *know* about what You have done?" the angel asked. "How will Your Good News be spread, Lord? Did You leave behind a strong organization on earth? Are there some well-defined plans for letting the people You love know that You died for them?"

The Savior's answer surprised—and frankly, disappointed—the angel. "No, I left no organization there. Only a small company of disciples, mostly of very humble birth. It is up to them to tell the world."

"But what if they fail You?" persisted Gabriel. "What plan do You have then?"

Gazing downward at the world He had just left—the world He so loved—Jesus replied, "I have no other plan."

The story is a legend. The conclusion is an inescapable challenge from the Word of God: "*You* will be my witnesses" (Acts 1:8, italics added). Not angelic messengers, not a religious organization. The work for which Jesus gave His life is in *our* hands, His everyday followers. He has no other plan. Heaven's lifesaving message for people who are dying has been entrusted to us: "*We* are . . . Christ's ambassadors, as though God were making His appeal through *us*" (2 Corinthians 5:20, italics added). "How, then, can they call on the one they have not believed in? And how can they believe in the one of whom they have not heard? And how can they hear without someone preaching to them?" (Romans 10:14–15).

For some person you know, some person you care about, that "someone" is you. You have been positioned by God where you are to be the face and the voice of Jesus to the people around you. Just as Satan has blinded their eyes to their eternal danger, he may have blinded you as well. Just as Satan has kept them from Jesus by preoccupying them with themselves, he may have kept you from Jesus' mission with a plateful of personal issues and "earth stuff." He knows his hold on his prisoners is tentative, lasting only until they die. In order to hold onto them, he must keep the rescuers from seeing both the lostness of those around them and their own lifesaving role. If Satan's prisoners should ever see and hear Jesus through His ambassadors, the Enemy knows they would run to the Cross and be lost to him forever.

A SPIRITUAL HUNGER FOR MORE

But Jesus will not let those who were meant to be His rescuers be content in a self-focused faith or spiritual passivity. He makes them hungry for more. He's made *you* hungry for more. That's why nothing you've accomplished or acquired has answered your soul's restlessness for a greater significance. This is the call to greatness. Jesus has been "causing you to hunger" (Deuteronomy 8:3) so you would be ready for His call to join Him in His lifesaving mission, to "seek and to save what was lost" (Luke 19:10).

Or to bring it down to the world you live in, to "seek and to save" _____ (the name of someone close to you) who is lost.

Because you have been created with "eternity in your heart," your heart has been restless for a life on earth that has a lot more that's eternal—like helping people around you be in heaven with you forever! All God has given you—your relationships, your position, your talents, your resources, your home, your life experiences—they all become "eternalized" when they are turned toward rescuing the people for whom the Son of God gave His life.

Until you answer the summons of Jesus to join Him in "bringing many sons to glory" (Hebrews 2:10), the holy restlessness in your heart will not go away. But when you see the "dyingness" of the people around you, when you let Jesus break your heart for them, when you commit yourself each new day to look for and go for spiritual rescue opportunities—that is when you will begin to experience the fulfillment, the exhilaration known only by those who are doing what they were *reborn* to do. You are answering your Savior's call to greatness—to help dying people change their eternal address from hell to heaven.

Just last weekend, my friend Bill heard me talk about "making the greatest possible difference with the rest of your life." He came to me afterward and with moist eyes said, "Would you please pray for me? I want that." We stopped and prayed right there that God would, even that very week, give him a chance to do something really eternal.

That was on Sunday. On Tuesday, Bill called me and reported with evident excitement that "the prayer you prayed for me Sunday is working already!" Bill had long been spiritually concerned for Mike, a man who rents office space from him. Mike left his Jewish faith at the age of twelve and had basically not been interested in God, or even sure of His existence, since then. Until that week. When Mike asked Bill about his weekend, my friend had a natural opportunity to recount some of the exciting things he had seen God do. And, for once, Mike wanted to know more; he said he was really looking for inner peace. God had opened a door . . . He opened a lost man's heart . . . then he opened Bill's mouth. Christ's ambassador to Mike gently shared with him the peace Jesus died to give us.

Then Mike asked if he could borrow Bill's Bible. "I'm going to start reading it every day, and I'm going to pray before I read it and say, 'God, if You're real, show Yourself to me as I read this book.'" I think we know how God will respond.

My friend Bill knew the restlessness in his heart could only be satisfied by something eternal—by making an eternal difference in people's lives. And when he gave himself anew to that rescue mission of Jesus, God gave him both an eternity opportunity and the renewed joy of someone who is about his Master's business. He wants to do the same for you—over and over again.

"SOMETHING YOU CAN'T PUT A PRICE TAG ON"

In a matter of seconds in November of 1999, much of the Turkish city of Izmit was reduced to rubble by a killer earthquake. In that terrifying moment, countless people were suddenly buried under tons of twisted concrete and steel. And, as always in a disaster, lives depended on that one hope-giving imperative: *rescue*. Ordinary people instinctively began to plunge into the wreckage, desperately hoping to give someone a chance to live.

The cry for help was heard all the way from Turkey to Fairfax, Virginia, where a disaster rescue team responded immediately. Within forty-eight hours, they were on the ground in Turkey, ready to assist in the lifesaving effort. They worked tirelessly for several days and nights, finding a handful who are alive today because they brought them out. But they also found many who had died in the quake.

One of the Virginia rescuers was asked what kept them going when there was so much disappointment, so much death. His answer was passionate: "Until you've been part of a team that's saved someone's life, and seen the look on their face when they come out of the hole, you can't understand. It's something you can't put a price tag on."[1]

He's right. Especially when you have saved someone's life *forever*. The "hole" you've brought them out of is "the dominion of darkness" (Colossians 1:13) and what would have been, but for Christ's intervention through you, "everlasting destruction . . . shut out from the presence of the Lord" (2 Thessalonians 1:9). You really can't put a price tag on the deep, deep joy of being God's rescuer, of giving life to someone who might very well have died if you had not gone in for the rescue.

This very day, someone you know is in the water, dying outside the lifeboat of Jesus. For far too long, far too many of us who are rescued have just been rowing along in our lifeboats, either oblivious to the dying people outside or afraid to risk a rescue. But we cannot just let them die. Not when Jesus died so they wouldn't have to. It's time to turn your lifeboat around . . . to throw out a lifeline of hope and help. It's time to commit the rest of your years on earth to pulling in as many dying people as you can.

Someone loved you enough to pull you into the lifeboat. It's your turn now.

NOTES

Chapter 2: Your Personal Titanic

1. William Barclay, ed., *The Gospel of Matthew* (The Daily Study Bible Series), vol.2 (Philadelphia: Westminster, 1975), 378.

Chapter 6: Would You Like to Super-Size That?

1. V. Raymond Edman, *They Found the Secret* (Grand Rapids: Zondervan, 1960), 28.

2. J. Oswald Sanders, *Spiritual Leadership* (Chicago: Moody, 1980), 130–131; George Sweeting, "Principles for Praying," *Moody*, July/August 1992, 70.

Chapter 7: Thinking Lost

1. Charles Colson, "Reaching the Pagan Mind," *Christianity Today*, 9 November 1992, 112.

2. Eddie Gibbs, *Winning Them Back* (Kent, England: Monarch, 1993), 176.

3. "The Generation that Forgot God: The Baby Boom Goes Back to Church, and Church Will Never Be the Same," *Time*, 5 April 1993, cover; story by Richard N. Ostling on pages 44–49.

4. Doug LeBlanc, "Living in a Post-Christian Culture," *Moody*, June 1994, 12 .

5. Charles Nuckolls, "In Search of the Sacred," *Newsweek,* 11 November 1994, 55.

6. As quoted in David G. Meyers, "More Age of Plenty But Our Souls Are Empty," *Christianity Today,* 24 April 2000, 96.

7. Wade Clark Roof, "A Generation of Prodigals," *Christianity Today,* 25 October 1993, 94–95.

8. Alyssa Milano, *USA Today,* 1 March 2000, D1.

9. As quoted in Donald W. McCullough, *The Trivialization of God* (Colorado Springs: Nav-Press, 1995), 20.

Chapter 10: The Story Only You Can Tell

1. Payne Stewart, *Charisma,* January 2000, 27–28.

Chapter 11:"No Greater Honor"

1. "Asleep in the Light," by Keith Green. © 1979 Birdwing Music/BMG Songs, Inc./Ears To Hear Music. Used by permission.

2. Ron Hutchcraft, "Yours for Life" (Garland, Tex.: American Tract Society, 1998).

Chapter 13: Lifesaving Jesus' Way

1. Karl Menninger, *Whatever Became of Sin?* (New York: Hawthorn, 1973), 13.

2. Dan Rather, "On Lonely Streets," *48 Hours,* no date.

3. Fred Durst, *Parade,* 16 January 2000, 10.

4. "One Question," *USA Today,* Fall 1999, A1.

Chapter 14: Removing the Roadblocks

1. "Going for Higher Authority," *USA Today,* 9 February 2000, 18A.

2. Elizabeth C. Clephane, "The Ninety and Nine." In public domain.

Epilogue: Turning the Lifeboats Around

1. "The Big One," *Newsweek,* 30 August 1999, 25.

Steps to Peace with God

Step 1 God's Purpose:
Peace and Life

God loves you and wants you to experience peace and life—abundant and eternal.

The Bible Says . . .

"... we have peace with God through our Lord Jesus Christ." **Romans 5:1**

"For God so loved the world that He gave His only begotten Son, that whoever believes in Him should not perish but have everlasting life." **John 3:16**

"... I have come that they may have life, and that they may have it more abundantly." **John 10:10b**

Since God planned for us to have peace and the abundant life right now, why are most people not having this experience?

Step 2 Our Problem:
Separation

God created us in His own image to have an abundant life. He did not make us as robots to automatically love and obey Him, but gave us a will and a freedom of choice.

We chose to disobey God and go our own willful way. We still make this choice today. This results in separation from God.

Our choice results in separation from God.

The Bible Says . . .

"For all have sinned and fall short of the glory of God." **Romans 3:23**

"For the wages of sin is death, but the gift of God is eternal life in Christ Jesus our Lord." **Romans 6:23**

Our Attempts

Through the ages, individuals have tried in many ways to bridge this gap . . . without success . . .

The Bible Says . . .

"There is a way that seems right to man, but in the end it leads to death." Proverbs 14:12

"But your iniquities have separated you from God; and your sins have hidden His face from you, so that He will not hear." Isaiah 59:2

There is only one remedy for this problem of separation.

Step 3 God's Remedy: The Cross

Jesus Christ is the only answer to this problem. He died on the Cross and rose from the grave, paying the penalty for our sin and bridging the gap between God and people.

The Bible Says . . .

". . . God is on one side and all the people on the other side, and Christ Jesus, Himself man, is between them to bring them together . . ." 1 Timothy 2:5

"For Christ also has suffered once for sins, the just for the unjust, that He might bring us to God . . ." 1 Peter 3:18a

"But God demonstrates His own love for us in this: While we were still sinners, Christ died for us." Romans 5:8

God has provided the only way . . . we must make the choice . . .

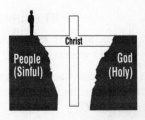

Step 4 Our Response: Receive Christ

We must trust Jesus Christ and receive Him by personal invitation.

The Bible Says . . .

"Behold, I stand at the door and knock. If anyone hears My voice and opens the door, I will come in to him and dine with him, and he with Me." Revelation 3:20

"But as many as received Him, to them He gave the right to become children of God, even to those who believe in His name." John 1:12

". . . if you confess with your mouth the Lord Jesus and believe in your heart that God has raised Him from the dead, you will be saved." Romans 10:9

Are you here . . . or here?

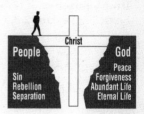

Is there any good reason why you cannot receive Jesus Christ right now?

How to receive Christ:

1. Admit your need (I am a sinner).
2. Be willing to turn from your sins (repent).
3. Believe that Jesus Christ died for you on the Cross and rose from the grave.
4. Through prayer, invite Jesus Christ to come in and control your life through the Holy Spirit. (Receive Him as Lord and Savior.)

What to Pray:

Dear Lord Jesus,

I know that I am a sinner and need Your forgiveness. I believe that You died for my sins. I want to turn from my sins. I now invite You to come into my heart and life. I want to trust and follow You as Lord and Savior.

In Jesus' name. Amen.

_____   _____
Date   Signature

God's Assurance: His Word

If you prayed this prayer,

The Bible Says...

"For 'whoever calls upon the name of the Lord will be saved.'" **Romans 10:13**

Did you sincerely ask Jesus Christ to come into your life? Where is He right now? What has He given you?

"For it is by grace you have been saved, through faith—and this is not from yourselves, it is the gift of God—not by works, so that no one can boast." Ephesians 2:8,9

The Bible Says...

"He who has the Son has life; he who does not have the Son of God does not have life. These things I have written to you who believe in the name of the Son of God, that you may know that you have eternal life, and that you may continue to believe in the name of the Son of God." **1 John 5:12–13, NKJV**

Receiving Christ, we are born into God's family through the supernatural work of the Holy Spirit who indwells every believer...this is called regeneration or the "new birth."

This is just the beginning of a wonderful new life in Christ. To deepen this relationship you should:

1. Read your Bible every day to know Christ better.
2. Talk to God in prayer every day.
3. Tell others about Christ.
4. Worship, fellowship, and serve with other Christians in a church where Christ is preached.
5. As Christ's representative in a needy world, demonstrate your new life by your love and concern for others.

God bless you as you do.

Billy Graham

If you want further help in the decision you have made, write to:
Billy Graham Evangelistic Association P.O. Box 779, Minneapolis, Minnesota 55440-0779